Homespun

Teaching Local History in Grades 6–12

Robert L. Stevens

HEINEMANN
Portsmouth, NH

Heinemann
A division of Reed Elsevier Inc.
361 Hanover Street
Portsmouth, NH 03801–3912
www.heinemann.com

Offices and agents throughout the world

The author and publisher wish to thank those who have generously given permission to reprint borrowed material:

Activities in Chapters 2, 3, 4, and 8 were adapted from *Middle Grades Social Studies: Teaching and Learning for Active and Responsible Citizenship* by Michael G. Allen and Robert L. Stevens. Copyright © 1994 by Allyn & Bacon. Adapted by permission.

Figures 5–5, 9–1, and 9–2—Art by Seymour Fogel reproduced by permission of Jared Fogel.

"A Walk Through Time" by Alice Aud, Gini Bland, and Barbara Brown was first published in *Middle Level Learning,* September 1999. Copyright © 1999 by the National Council for the Social Studies. Reprinted by permission.

The cover of "Old Hometown" is reprinted with permission of Melinda Beckett.

"The Real World: Community Speakers in the Classroom" by Lindy G. Poling was first published in *Middle Level Learning,* May/June 2000. Copyright © 2000 by the National Council for the Social Studies. Reprinted with permission.

"Actual and Virtual Reality: Making the Most of Field Trips" by Geoffrey Scheurman was first published in *Social Education,* January 1998. Copyright © 1998 by the National Council for the Social Studies. Reprinted with permission.

"Doing Real History: Citing Your Mother in Your Research Paper" by Andrea Libresco was first published in *Social Education,* January/February 2001. Copyright © 2001 by the National Council for the Social Studies. Reprinted with permission.

Library of Congress Cataloging-in-Publication Data
Stevens, Robert L., 1944–
   Homespun : teaching local history in grades 6–12 / Robert L. Stevens.
     p.   cm.
   Includes bibliographical references.
   ISBN 0-325-00334-1 (acid-free paper)
   1. United States—History, Local—Study and teaching. I. Title.

E175.8 .S79   2001
973'.071'273—dc21

              2001024959

Editor: William Varner
Production: Elizabeth Valway
Cover design: Jenny Jensen Greenleaf, Greenleaf Illustration & Design
Manufacturing: Louise Richardson

Printed in the United States of America on acid-free paper
05 04 03 02 01 DA 1 2 3 4 5

This book is dedicated to Julie, who not only dances well, but is highly creative when teaching science and social studies.

Contents

Acknowledgments
ix

Introduction
xi

PART I

Chapter One
Getting Started
1

Chapter Two
**Gravestones, Cemeteries, Markers,
and Historic Sites**
12

Chapter Three
Write a History
35

Chapter Four
The American House
48

Chapter Five
Using Primary Sources
60

Chapter Six
Oral History
76

Chapter Seven
**How to Get from Here to There:
Maps and Their Uses**
83

Chapter Eight
Write Your Family History
90

Chapter Nine
Create a Community Image
113

Chapter Ten
Order in the Court: Field Trip Liability
125

PART II

Chapter Eleven
**"'A Walk Through Time': A Living History Project"
Screven County Middle School, Sylvania, Georgia**
133

Chapter Twelve
**"Old Hometown,"
School District of Escambia, Pensacola, Florida**
138

Chapter Thirteen
**"The Real World:
Community Speakers in the Classroom,"
Milbrook High School, Raleigh, North Carolina**
146

Chapter Fourteen
**"Actual and Virtual Reality:
Making the Most of Field Trips,"
Fort Snelling Historic Site, St. Paul, Minnesota**
154

Chapter Fifteen
**"Doing REAL History:
Citing Your Mother in Your Research Paper,"
Oceanside High School, New York**
163

Appendix A: The Turner Thesis
171

Acknowledgments

First and foremost, I want to thank Bill Varner, editor at Heinemann, for inviting me to write *Homespun*. Although I had submitted a proposal for another subject, my vita revealed I not only had an interest in local history but had taught it for many years at Rye Junior High School in Rye, New Hampshire.

It was at Rye where Principal Gregory Kendall supported the many hands-on activities and field trips I wanted my students to be engaged in as they learned about their community. During those years from 1978 to 1985, I received the support of parents and the interest of my students. In 1990, the New England League of Middle Schools published *Gavels to Gravestones*, a monograph that presented some of my early teaching activities. Between 1994 and today, the editors of *Social Education*, Michael Simpson and Jennifer Rothwell, have assisted me in the preparation of many manuscripts, some of which appear in this text. I have always appreciated their comments and suggestions.

Since working on this text, I have had support and assistance from many friends and colleagues. Donna Colson deserves my deepest gratitude for her typing and formatting skills. In spite of the NCATE accreditation visit and program reviews, she continued to press forward on this manuscript. I was very pleased to receive from Dale and Jean Clatterbuck family letters and news accounts of the death of T. K. West, which are found in Chapter 8, "Write Your Family History." Thanks to William Cahill, U.S. Navy, retired, an old friend and intrepid amateur Civil War historian, for the many walks through the Virginia, Maryland, and Pennsylvania battle sites and to Missy, who provided all the recovery dinners. And finally, thanks to Woody and Tish Woodruff, who lent me all of their histories of Candler and Emanuel Counties in Georgia, as well as their knowledge of events long past.

Introduction

The teaching of history has been criticized recently. "American history in the past has been written from the top down, an approach feasible enough as long as scholars were content to write only political and diplomatic history," Constance Greene reminds us (1940, 275). As teachers, our problem is that we work with nonscholars, twelve to eighteen years of age—immature learners, to use Dewey's definition. Because of the way history is generally written and taught, it lacks the richness of content that creates excitement for the young mind. We often suffer from the fact that we either dumb down history to accommodate slow learners or cover the waterfront in a safe but sterile approach that satisfies the need for accountability (because we've covered the content) but does little to instill an appreciation for, or a fundamental understanding of, history. In either case, it lacks appeal.

Local history offers a way out of some of these problems. It is the lifeblood of a community, imbued with traditions, beliefs, social and economic forces, religions, and ethnicities that are stitched together like a quilt. And like a quilt, it provides a pattern that has meaning. It also provides a multiperspective approach to understanding history. Each community in the United States developed at different times along different lines and, therefore, represents different populations and cultural inheritances. Moreover, each community is framed by geographical limitations, limitations that afford each community its uniqueness. For example, Eastern seaboard communities developed differently than frontier settlements; natural resources determined the character of each area as well as the introduction of specific technologies. This uniqueness gives students a personal, meaningful connection to the local history curriculum.

Foundation for a Local History Curriculum

My interest in local history began in 1956 when I entered the sixth grade at the Rye Center School in Rye, New Hampshire. I was taught by three excellent social studies teachers, Mrs. Sykes, Mr. Luther, and

Mr. Ladd, whose passion for history made me and my classmates want to learn. One's mind is easily drawn to the past when growing up in a place like Rye. Riding past the old family cemeteries on bicycles, playing in the eighteenth-century homes of friends, and listening to stories about the Isle of Shoals from my great-grandparents created a historical sense of place. History had a long reach and pulled me in. But it was good teaching that created the opportunities that I continue to pursue to this day.

I believe it is extremely important to capture the imagination of middle and secondary students through activity-based history lessons. Cultivating the imagination is critical to helping learners understand local history; it is their only vehicle to make sense of the past. I have found that field trips, museum visits, artifacts and documents, and stories can all be used to evoke the past through sights, smells, sounds, and touch.

As a framework for helping students understand their own history and develop a historical imagination, I use three of the National Council for the Social Studies Curriculum Standards (1994):

II: Time, Continuity, and Change. *Social studies programs should include experiences that provide for the study of the ways human beings view themselves in and over time.* Teaching local history helps students answer the following questions. Who am I?, What happened in the past?, and How am I connected to those in the past? Answering these powerful questions helps students reconstruct the past and at the same time develop a historical perspective.

III: Peoples, Places, and Environments. *Social studies programs should include experiences that provide for the study of people, places, and environments.* The study of local geography helps students answer the following questions. Where are things located?, Why are they located where they are?, and What patterns are reflected in the grouping of things? This area helps students make informed decisions about the relationship between human beings and the environment.

IV: Individual Development and Identity. *Social studies programs should include experiences that provide for the study of individual development and identity.* This standard helps students answer the following questions. How do culture, groups, and institutions influence personal identity? To what extent do local values influence student behavior? This helps students view themselves in relation to their local history. In addition, I use the five fundamental geographic themes—location, place, human environmental interaction, movement, and region (Geography for Life 1994)—to help students analyze local history problems.

The value of the NCSS and Geography for Life standards is that they can be used to analyze the uniqueness of a place in time, a place that students know so well because they live there. This affords them a richness of experience due to their familiarity with the physical environment and the people. Students' perceptions of themselves, like noted sociologist Cooley's "looking glass self," are reflections in the mirror of the community. We all develop a sense of self and identity partially because of where we live. That sense of place is created through the interaction of historical, social-psychological, and geographical forces. However, many of our students are products of a mobile society—a rootless society, some would argue. Therefore, helping students develop a sense of place through an understanding of local history is not only academically defensible but, in terms of their social-psychological development, critical as well.

In addition, local history is a microcosm of national history. The life of a local community very often is affected by national events. The reactions of citizens and institutions provide insights into our national character. "In short, local history personalizes an often impersonal subject" (Mahoney 1981, 9). It is through teaching local history that broader perspectives can be taught in a meaningful way.

I designed my local history activities to be meaningful based on the educational theory of John Dewey. In 1902, Dewey cited three areas that create problems between the student and the curriculum: (1) the narrow but personal world of the child against the impersonal but infinitely extended world of time and space; (2) the unity, the single wholeheartedness of the child's life against the specialization and divisions of the curriculum; and (3) an abstract principle of logical classification and arrangement against the practical and emotional bonds of child life. I find these observations just as valid today. The activities I present in this text attempt to bridge the gap between the history curriculum and the world of the child, which is by definition immature and underdeveloped, with an appreciation of certain "social aims, meanings, and values incarnate in the matured experience of any adult" (Dewey 1902, 2). The focus is the student who lives in a parochial world of immediate friends, family, and community and who is not concerned with abstract concepts, facts, and laws—a Tom Sawyer, if you will. As teachers, we need to use the student's experience as a starting point for learning new material. Local history presents material close at hand: the family, the neighborhood, and the community. "The child and the curriculum are simply two limits which define a single process" (Dewey 1902, 2).

My teaching, supervision, and museum experience have made two things clear: first, students need to be interested and engaged in any learning activity, and second, the curriculum has to be organized to avoid confusion and produce consistency. The materials and approach should be student centered; after all, they are the learners.

About This Book

In 1990, the New England League of Middle Schools published *Gavels to Gravestones: Seven Middle School Social Studies Activities,* in which I described several student-centered activities designed to bring the past alive for students. This first publication was an outgrowth of my graduate education at the University of Massachusetts–Amherst, two years as Assistant Professor of Education at Washington College, Maryland, two years' experience working at Strawbery Banke Historical Museum in Portsmouth, New Hampshire and seven years of teaching junior high school social studies. This new text is going to expand on some of those early successful activities and combine them with additional activities I developed while teaching social studies teachers at the University of Wisconsin–Stevens Point and currently at Georgia Southern University. In addition, I am most excited to share with you a number of local history lessons and projects that have been published in *Social Education* and which support my teaching ideas and will provide you additional resources as you develop local history units. These are presented in two ways: some of the lessons I combine with my own teaching strategies because of the natural curriculum fit and others are showcased in Part II because of the nature of the projects. Each chapter is organized to describe specific instructional strategies related to teaching local history. As you become aware of the variety of possibilities, I hope you will see how the book is interconnected. For instance, in Chapter 2, the focus is on gravestones, cemeteries, and historic sites. Several other chapters, such as Chapter 5, "Using Primary Sources," Chapter 8, "Write Your Family History," and Chapter 9, "Create a Community Image," have activities that can be used in conjunction with Chapter 2.

Chapter 1, "Getting Started," is simply a primer to help you if you have not taught a local history unit or series of lessons before. It will show you how to quickly create an initial framework for teaching about your local area.

Chapter 2, "Gravestones, Cemeteries, Markers, and Historic Sites," provides many student-centered activities using primary sources to help students become local historians.

Chapter 3, "Write a History," suggests possible starting points to help students decide which topics should be included in a local history, conduct historical research, and effectively use elements essential to good writing.

Chapter 4, "The American House," provides activities that will help students understand architectual and housing patterns in their local community.

Chapter 5, "Using Primary Sources," demonstrates how photography is used to teach students about the coal industry in Harlan, Kentucky.

Chapter 6, "Oral History," suggests strategies for helping students conduct interviews with family members as well as others who have witnessed history in the making.

Chapter 7, "How to Get from Here to There," shows how maps can be used to interpret local history. Maps of Salem, Massachusetts, during the 1690 witchcraft trials reveal the relationship between local values and accused witches.

Chapter 8, "Write Your Family History," shows not only how to research a family geneology but also how to create lessons that place family members in the context of history itself.

Chapter 9, "Create a Community Image," is a culminating activity that draws on students' creative potential to portray their local community to the world.

Chapter 10, "Order in the Court," presents tort liability in a clear, concise manner for use when you are conducting a field trip.

Part II is a collection of local projects and activities that represent best practice in helping students to learn about their own local history. These local history programs have won awards in their respective states or have been published in *Social Education*, the journal for the National Council for the Social Studies. I hope these model activities will help you create projects that reflect your community's history.

In this text I want to convey the interest in local history I enjoyed with Mrs. Sykes, Mr. Ladd, and Mr. Luther and how I conveyed that same interest to my students. I also want to show you what I taught and how I taught it and discuss some of the problems and obstacles I overcame while teaching it. It is my hope that this will help you think about ways to teach a local history course or unit and provide you with some ideas to try with your students to help them take a journey into the past.

References

Conrad, J. A. 1989. *Developing Local History Programs in Community Libraries*. Chicago: Chicago American Library Association.

Curriculum Standards for the Social Studies. 1994. Washington, D.C.: National Council for the Social Studies.

Geography for Life: National Geography Standards. 1994. Washington, D.C.: National Geographic Research & Exploration.

Greene, C. M. 1940. "The Value of Local History," in C. F. Ware, *The Cultural Approach to History* New York: Columbia University Press.

Kammen, C. ed.. 1996. *The Pursuit of Local History: Readings on Theory and Practice.* Walnut Creek, CA: Altermira.

Mahoney, J. 1981. *Local History: A Guide for Research and Writing.* Washington, D.C.: NEA.

PART I

Chapter One

Getting Started

Every fall for years I looked forward to teaching my local history unit, From Sandy Beach to the Present. I looked forward to it because it excited my students. Within a few days of beginning the unit, they all wanted to know more about their small community—its history, what happened where and to whom. The close proximity to cemeteries with inscribed stones telling their owners' stories, center-chimney Colonials whose windows witnessed history, stone walls separating field from forest, and the old town hall repository of original deeds and tax records invited my students to "do" history. Every year I was able to create more activities and opportunities for extended research.

But how does a teacher who has never taught a local history unit or created a lesson from local lore begin? Though each local history unit is entirely unique, there are some basic approaches that will help you get started. The key to creating a good local history unit is planning. Before I taught my first local history unit, I had to decide when to teach it and where in the curriculum was the most appropriate time to teach it. For me, it was almost as soon as school started in the fall. Our town, Rye, New Hampshire, originally Sandy Beach, was settled in 1623. I focused on the early years of Rye while teaching about the Colonial period. It was a natural curriculum fit; throughout the remainder of the year, I would teach a lesson or create an activity that coincided with other periods in United States history, thus integrating local and national history. When will you teach your local history unit? That is entirely up to you. For instance, if you teach in California, you might introduce your local unit during a study of the 1848 gold rush or you might decide to begin much earlier when California was populated with native peoples who witnessed the arrival of the early Spanish.

Whenever you decide to teach local history, it will generate a great deal of interest because your students are close to it.

Next, you will need to assemble as many resources as possible regarding your community's past. William P. Filby's *Directory of American Libraries with Genealogy or Local History Collections* is an excellent first source because it lists all the libraries in the United States that house local history collections. For example, imagine you are a teacher in Emanuel County, Georgia, and you want to create a local history unit for your eighth-grade Georgia history class. You consult Filby's directory and see it lists the Ohoopee Regional Library, John E. Ladson Jr. Genealogical and Historical Foundation Library Branch. Among the many resources in that library, you find *Footprints Along the Hoopee: A History of Emanuel County, 1812–1900,* by James E. Dorsey (1978). You open the book and locate the table of contents. It reads as follows:

Chapter I: The Setting

Chapter II: The Early Settlers

Chapter III: Institutions and Social Classes

Chapter IV: The Civil War

Chapter V: Reconstruction

Chapter VI: Progress and Growth

Here you have an excellent starting point to begin planning your unit. When I taught my first unit on Rye, I consulted Parson's *History of Rye 1623–1903* (1905). The table of contents helped me create a framework to begin teaching Rye's early history.

Another possibility is to ask your students to list what they don't know about their community on the board. The list will generate a lot of possible research topics, such as the following:

I don't know . . .

Why our town was settled.

Who the founder was.

What life was like during the nineteenth century.

What the first schools were like.

What the first settlers did for a living.

What the death rate was in Colonial times.

If natural disasters ever affected our community.

This list will go on until all the possibilities have been exhausted. One of my classes generated fifty-four areas of investigation. This allows your students to create their own topics for investigation (see Chapter 3, "Write a History").

Once you have established an outline for your unit of study or a list of topics, the next step is to create activities for each lesson. Here again, what you or your students select should reflect your community's local history. The following list of local resources will help you identify possible activities you can develop for and perhaps with your students. After all, we want them to become local historians.

Local Resources

School Records

Today's students have an immense curiosity about what schools were like long ago. They can investigate financial records, discipline referrals, and teachers' contracts to begin to understand the nature of education in the nineteenth century. I have come across the following examples while conducting my own research into this topic.

In Emanuel County, Georgia, students attended school from between three and six months each year at a cost of five cents per day per pupil instructed. One school's expense list for 1826 reveals the following:

Books, paper and ink stands

Young Man's Companion

Spelling book

Bottle of ink

Discipline has been a perennial concern of parents and educators. School vandalism is not just a current problem. Students will enjoy researching historical applications of this problem. In my study on Emanuel County in the 1890s, I discovered that four school buildings that students were responsible for were burned to the ground.

> There have been four incendiary burnings of school houses in the 49th district within the past four months. Almost as soon as a new building is completed, the fire bug applies a torch to it. The good people of that community should apprehend the perpetrators of these outrages, and nothing would be too bad for them. (Dorsey 1978, 170)

In another case I have researched, I found that students in Pittsfield, New Hampshire, created many problems for their community. An anecdote from the *History of Pittsfield* describes an extreme situation:

> For thirty years this house stood at the corner, and then it was taken apart and moved to the eastern slope of Catamount on Berry Road, where it was settled on a ledge which provided a firm foundation for the front of the building, while the rear was supported by posts, as the

ground fell rapidly toward the steep ravine but a few feet distant. A little later this precarious position proved too much of a temptation to the less academic minded pupils. One noon hour, while the teacher was away for her lunch, the boys knocked out the blocking out from under the rear of the building and before she returned they had almost succeeded in levering the whole schoolhouse into the deep ravine behind it. That did it! The teacher dismissed school and rallied the parents, who, after a short conference, decided to move the building across the road and down the hill a short distance where it was set up again, this time on a more level spot and on a firmer foundation. Here, surrounded by a stone wall on three sides, it remained, without any untoward incidents until 1862. In that year, the scholars being dissatisfied with the performance of the current teacher, one spring day pushed her outside and proceeded to wreck the interior of the building. After the damage was appraised, it was decided to discontinue school that year; nor was school held the next. (Young 1952, 254)

Hopefully, not all students behaved the way these two examples suggest. Another related area of early schooling that today's students can research is what types of discipline were administered and for what offenses.

Schools reflect community attitudes and values. Even today, the lives of teachers are subject to community scrunity. School boards expect teachers to behave above the norm, to serve as moral examples. Examples of teaching contracts and behavior codes help us gain insights into local community expectations. Louis Fischer and David Schimmel (1973, 2–5) illustrate conditions of employment for teachers in their book *The Rights of Students and Teachers*. Excerpts from a 1920 teaching contract reveal teachers as second-class citizens:

I promise to take a vital interest in all phases of Sunday work, donating of my time, service, and money without stint for the uplift and benefit of the community.

I promise to abstain from all dancing, immodest dressing, and any other conduct unbecoming a teacher and a lady.

I promise not to go out with any young men except in so far as it may be necessary to stimulate Sunday work.

I promise not to fall in love, to become engaged or secretly married.

I promise not to encourage or tolerate the least familiarity on the part of any of my boy pupils.

I promise to sleep at least eight hours a night, to eat carefully, and to take every precaution to keep in the best of health and spirits, in order that I may be better able to render efficient service to my pupils.

I promise to remember that I owe a duty to the townspeople who are paying me my wages, that I owe respect to the school board and the superintendent that hired me, and that I shall consider myself at all times the willing servant of the school board and the townspeople.

In addition, the contract specified the following restrictions:

▪ *Drinking.* Although in colonial times teachers drank alcoholic beverages quite openly, the later temperance movement brought severe and lasting restrictions. Drunkenness almost certainly cost a teacher his or her job, and applicants for positions usually faced the questions, "Do you drink?" and "Do you smoke?" Contracts forbade drinking and smoking, and even an occasional drink in a private home could lead to chastisement or dismissal. As in most other restrictions, small towns were more severe than cities, and the Northeast was less restrictive than other parts of the country.

▪ *Smoking.* The use of tobacco, particularly by women, was frowned upon. In many places this was a specifically forbidden practice whose violation led to dismissal. There are schools today that will not hire women who smoke, and many states still require teachers to teach the "evil effects of smoking and alcohol."

▪ *Theater.* It comes as a surprise to many that theater attendance was a forbidden form of amusement in many communities. In fact, such restrictions lasted until about 1920.

▪ *Dancing.* Dancing and card playing were frowned upon even more than attending the theater. In connection with any socially marginal or questionable behavior, a much higher degree of abstinence was required of teachers than of their pupil's parents.

▪ *Divorce.* Divorce would generally lead to dismissal and a change of profession. "After all, divorce is immoral, and you don't want an immoral teacher influencing your children." Gambling and swearing were similarly treated.

▪ *Marriage.* Oddly enough, marriage could also lead to dismissal, particularly in the case of women teachers. Until the 1920s and 1930s, contracts tended to prohibit marriage, but later these were eliminated as unreasonable and against public policy.

▪ *Sexual immorality.* Sexual immorality was almost always disastrous. Whether it consisted of adultery or fornication, or even rumors of such conduct, dismissal would follow.

▪ *Late hours.* Going out on a school night or staying out until late at night was forbidden. In fact, "keeping company" was against the rules in many communities, whereas others specified in their contracts that a woman teacher might "keep company" with only one man and that he might not be another teacher.

▪ *Gossip.* Rumor or gossip, however unfounded, tended to be sufficient for dismissal, particularly if it were related to sexual immorality. Since a teacher was expected to be a model adult, she could be dismissed if her *reputation* for good character was tarnished.

▪ *Publicity.* If the behavior of a teacher brought any unfavorable publicity to the school, his or her career was in jeopardy. Any unconventional behavior or nonconformity was treated as sufficient evidence of immaturity, instability, or immorality.

▪ *Grooming.* The personal appearance of the teachers was closely controlled. Cosmetics, gay colors, bobbed hair, sheer stockings, short skirts, low-cut dresses, and the like, were forbidden.

▪ *Racism.* White teachers, particularly in small communities, were dismissed if they were seen in public with blacks or visited their homes. In the South, white school boards would ignore sexual behavior on the part of black teachers that would lead to the dismissal of white teachers.

▪ *Organizations.* Membership in organizations was a very sensitive matter with many local variations. For example, in some communities teachers had to join the Ku Klux Klan to keep their job. In others, membership in the KKK led to immediate dismissal. There were many controversial and therefore "unsafe" organizations, including the American Civil Liberties Union. Teachers were not to take part in open, public criticism of issues, leaders, or organizations. The widely accepted exercise of free speech, press, or assembly was denied them. Any type of activity related to labor organizations was discouraged, and membership in a teachers' union would typically lead to dismissal.

How did your local community view teachers' behavior? Generally, cities were less restrictive than rural areas. Rural communities tended to keep a watchful eye on their teachers. Students could compare teaching contracts today with contracts drawn at the turn of the twentieth century and before. Do today's contracts reflect the local mores of a community?

Birth and Death Records

Students will be surprised when they study early birth and death records. They will find that infant mortality was extremely high in the eighteenth and nineteenth centuries. It was not uncommon for a woman in the 1840s to birth ten children, only to see two survive the age of majority. And on the other end of the spectrum, they will likewise be surprised to learn what a typical estate consisted of. In 1814, Ailia Padget died and left the following estate:

Two minor slaves $700.00

One stack of fodder 8.00

Two beds 50.00

A rifle 7.00

Desk 14.00

One cart 14.00

Kitchen utensils 12.00

1/2 bu. salt 1.75

One plow 2.00

3 hoes .... 50¢

Spinning wheel .... 75¢

Four deck of cards.............................. 2.00

Nineteen bu. of potatoes 4.75

300 acres of swampland 300.00

400 acres of pineland 200.00

Church Records

Churches were built soon after early settlement in most communities and their impact was felt immediately. These early churches not only prescribed rules of conduct but enforced them as well. Those who strayed from the path were censured. An examination of early records will help students understand local social mores and behavior expectations. An early transgression in a Georgian church reveals the accused "guilty first of indulging and encouraging disorder in his family, second for showing foul play in time of combat, third for falsehood, fourth for indulging theft committed by his Negro, for which the church expelled him from fellowship of this church" (Dorsey 1978, 38).

Census Records

What was your community like in 1880, and how do you know? Students who examine census records can create a social profile of their community. One entry from *The 1880 Census of Emanuel County, Georgia* provides the data necessary to create such a profile. Students can randomly select a cross-section of the population and then draw up the profile. Here is a list of information you could include in the profile, followed by a sample profile entry.

1. The name of each person whose place of abode on first day of June 1880 was in this family
2. Color: white—W; black—B; mulatto—MU; Chinese—C; or Indian—I
3. Sex: male—M; female—F

4. Age
5. Relationship of each person to head of family
6. Civil condition: single—S; married—M; widowed—W; or divorced—D
7. Profession, occupation, or trade: works on farm—WOF
8. Place of birth of this person
9. Place of birth of father of this person/Place of birth of mother of this person

Entry 236

1	2	3	4	5	6	7	8	9
Claban Fields	W	M	48		M	turpentine bus	NC	NC/NC
Ida	W	F	28	wife	M	at house		
Lutha E.	W	M	14	son		school	NC	NC/NC
Francis E.	W	F	11	dau		school	NC	NC/NC
Henry J.	W	M	8	son		school	NC	NC/NC
Maggie	W	F	5	dau				
Ellen Pierce	W	F	23	boarder		boarder		
Samuel Daniels	W	M	21	boarder		boarder		
Jessie Bryant	B	M	21	boarder		turpentine hand		
Warren C. Hodges	MU	M	20	boarder		works at still		

Photographs

The old adage "A picture is worth a thousand words" is relevant when using photographs to teach local history. Pictures provide documentary evidence of the history, the geography, and the social life of the past. Joseph M. Kirman (1995) suggests the following general questions to help guide discussion and inquiry when using photographs to understand local history. Students can answer the questions by comparing old and new photographs of the same scenes or area.

1. How has the scene changed?
2. Is the change for better or worse?
3. What is in the modern photograph that is in the earlier photograph?
4. What is in the modern photograph that could never be in the earlier photograph?

5. If you were in charge of developing this area from the date of the early photograph, would you have done anything different than what is shown in the modern photograph?

6. What type of lifestyle does the earlier photograph represent? How do you know?

7. What type of lifestyle does the modern photograph represent? How do you know?

8. What type of environmental impact do the older and newer photographs show?

9. Is anything being done in the old photograph that would not be permitted today, or anything being done in the modern photograph that would not have been permitted in earlier times? (11–13)

See my Teaching with Pictures activities in Chapter 5 for additional ideas.

Buildings (Architectural Styles)

"The United States possesses an impressive number of great structures from periods of the nation's history, plus many little-known but rewarding examples of regional and vernacular architecture" (Smith 1976, 7). From the Lady Pepperrel House in Kittery Point, Maine (1760), to the Governor Goodwin Mansion (1811), the Macpheadris-Warner House (1723), and the Wentworth-Gardner House (1760) in Portsmouth, New Hampshire, to the Palace of the Governors (1612) in Santa Fe, New Mexico, to the relatively modern design of Frank Lloyd Wright's Hollyhock (Barnsdall) House (1920) in Los Angeles, California, you will have unlimited opportunities to visit not only famous American homes but also vernacular homes, which are just as important to the study of local history. In Chapter 4, I present several activities to help students understand building styles in their communities.

Cemeteries

From the exotic pyramids of ancient Egypt to the cemeteries of today, burial sites capture the imaginations of students. My Rye students' first activity outside the classroom was to create a social profile of the community from their investigation of one of the local cemeteries. Rye has at least thirty-seven family cemeteries. The inscriptions from the most primitive to the most ornate tell us who our ancestors were, what they did, and when they lived. In the process of investigating gray slate headstones in a cemetery, my students learned a lot of local history. In

Chapter 2, I present activities ranging from the analysis of a single headstone to an investigation of historic sites.

Oral History

Every year I taught local history, I asked each of my students to invite a grandparent to visit class and tell us what life was like when he or she was growing up. Although all of the interviews were interesting, one grandmother, Nana Rand, was most memorable. Nana was in her eighties when she came to tell us about growing up on a farm in central New Hampshire. She brought with her a photograph of her six sisters and seven beautifully groomed black horses. The photograph created a stir in my students. It generated all sorts of questions and provided an excellent opportunity for them to learn about the past. In Chapter 6, "Oral History" and Chapter 8, "Write Your Family History," I present many activities to help you think about a variety of ways to use family members to help students connect with the past.

Other Resources

In addition to the local resources I just presented, there are many other possibilities:

1. Newspapers
2. Personal diaries and journals
3. Land transactions: recorder of deeds
4. Tax records
5. Marriage records
6. Military records
7. Local laws
8. Maps and charts
9. Museums

The rest of this book provides ideas and activities to capture the imagination and curiosity of your students. "Finding ways to stimulate the historical imagination involves them in the adventure of historical discovery, and acts as a stepping stone to more analytical forms of inquiry, such as the task of relating individuals and group lives in the past to the historical processes that were going on" (Simpson 1995, 3). Often while teaching, all I had to say was, "Look out the window across Washington Road and imagine Parson's Field two hundred years ago. Who is out there and what are they doing?" to get them off and running on meaningful historical investigations of their own.

References

Dorsey, J. E. 1978. *Footprints Along the Hoopee: A History of Emanuel County, 1812–1900.* Spartanburg, SC: Reprint.

1880 Census of Emanuel County, Georgia. 1880.

Emanuel Memories: 1776–1976. Swainsboro, GA: Swainsboro Forest-Blade.

Fischer, L., and D. Schimmel. 1973. *The Rights of Students and Teachers.* New York: Harper & Row.

Kirman, J. M. 1995. "Teaching About Local History Using Customized Photographs." *Social Education* 59 (1): 11–13.

Parsons, L. B. 1905. *History of Rye 1623–1903.* Concord, NH.

Simpson, M. 1995. "Teaching History Creatively." *Social Education* 59 (1): 3.

Smith, K. G. E. 1976. *A Pictorial History of Architecture in America.* New York: American Heritage.

Young, E. H. 1952. *History of Pittsfield, New Hampshire.* Concord, NH: New Hampshire Bindery.

Chapter Two

Gravestones, Cemeteries, Markers, and Historic Sites

"Upon the birth of a child, many families put away a cask of wine to be used for the offspring's wedding or funeral" (Wright and Hughes 1996, 239). In most cases, the funeral came first. From seventeenth-century graveyards found in eastern seaboard communities, to the garden-style cemeteries of the nineteenth century, to markers erected to commemorate historical events, students will find rich opportunities to learn local history.

Cemeteries and Gravestones

I planned cemetery activities to help my students become local historians. It was my task to help students create a picture of the past by carefully examining whatever clues the stones might offer. "The oldest and most persistent values are sometimes presented only in cemeteries" (Wright and Hughes 1996, ix).

I took my students to the cemetery in the fall, the best time of year to learn local history in New Hampshire. Not only did the field trips fit naturally into the curriculum because Rye was settled in 1623, but they occurred before the first cold snap foreshadowing winter and the nor'easters that would soon fill the cemetery with several feet of snow.

Luckily, Rye Junior High School was located near an old cemetery. I simply took my classes across Washington Road and through Parson's Field, and within minutes, we stood in the oldest section of the cemetery. I purposely selected the oldest section of the cemetery because it contained the most unusual stones, the ones I knew would fire my students' imagination. Lichen-covered, these old slates were tipped and sunken from years of New England freezes and thaws. The foundation of local society was framed like a jigsaw puzzle within these individual family plots.

The cemetery is the primer of a local history curriculum. It tells us who our ancestors were, what our ancestors did, where our ancestors came from, when our ancestors died, and why our ancestors died. The five Ws of a good story are all embedded in the local cemetery. Since I encourage my students to employ the basic five Ws of good news reporting when writing about their investigations (see Chapter 3), cemeteries are an excellent place to begin.

Who

From the earliest coastal communities on the Atlantic seaboard to the most recent suburban communities in twentieth-century America, the names of this nation's inhabitants are inscribed on their tombstones. Early New England slate headstones reveal Protestant English ancestry as well as the presence of the Native Americans who helped them survive the early years. The oldest graveyard in Rye has fourteen Native American markers. Scandinavian, German, and Polish surnames dominate stones in the upper Midwest, reflecting later immigration. As one moves from the old South, with its Scottish, Irish, and English surnames, into Louisiana, French names readily appear. These are soon replaced with Spanish inscriptions as one enters the Southwest. When the West opened and pioneers leapfrogged across the frontier, they left cemeteries and individual markers dotting the landscape behind them. Successive waves of immigrants created ethnic cemeteries that easily reveal who these people were. "From East to West, American ethnic patterns and values were literally cast in stone" (Stevens 1990).

What

Early inscriptions often tell the occupation, the social standing, and the family relation of the deceased. In cemeteries that have been preserved by local historical societies, you will find detailed information about famous and infamous persons.

Where

Discussing where the deceased came from is an excellent way to introduce the concept of push-pull factors of movement to your students. At any given time in history, communities will have an influx or an outflow of settlers. For example, in 1734, a group of Salzburgers came from Salzburg, Austria, to Savannah, Georgia, seeking religious freedom. They were Lutherans who sailed from Dover, England, on December 28, 1733, seeking refuge from religious persecution. General James Oglethorpe, founder of Savannah, established a German-speaking settlement north of Savannah as a buffer. Information such as this will help students determine what factors made their community grow or decline. In some communities, growth has remained stable for many generations. Back in the classroom, the preliminary findings from cemeteries can be analyzed to determine the growth patterns of the area.

When

The time that a person died can give us a clue about the reason he or she died. High rates of infant mortality will come as a surprise to most students. One day, while conducting cemetery research with a group of students, I heard several girls sobbing. They had found a stone that told of Mary Brown, who had died on Christmas Day in 1840. Two days later, her infant was also buried there. Clusters of death within the same year are very often the result of an epidemic. Yellow fever, malaria, and the great influenza epidemic of the 1920s can be ascertained by your students.

Why

Why and when a person died typically go hand in hand. Infant mortality and old age are the most obvious reasons death occurs, but accidents paint a picture of the times as well. Drownings and shipping accidents are engraved in coastal communities. Unusual deaths are also recorded. In 1824, the following death occurred in Rye, as described in the epitaph.

> Sheridan
> son of
> Jonathan Philbrick, Esq.
> & Sarah His Wife
> Was Instantly Killed
> by Lightening, While
> at School
> June 30, 1824
> Aged 11 Years

Many early stones recorded amusing epitaphs, such as these two:

Here lies Jane Smith, wife of Thomas Smith, Marble Cutter. This monument was erected by her husband as a tribute to her memory and a specimen of his handiwork. Monuments of this style are two hundred and fifty dollars.

Underneath this pile of stones lies all that's left of Sally Jones. Her name was Lord, it was not Jones, but Jones was used to rhyme with stones. (Mahoney 1981, 26)

Gravestones provide insights into community values of the past. Cemeteries help us understand individual and family attitudes toward death. The earliest headstones portrayed winged skulls and cherubs, symbolizing a medieval conception of death. Soon after the American Revolution, the willow and urn motif graced stones, symbolizing the new republic, a reference to Greek and Roman classical elements that represented the foundations of a democratic order. The newfound wealth and robber barrons of the Industrial Age witnessed rampant individualism. Monuments of death were erected to display people's status in life. Marble obelisks and highly ornate stones with animals dominated cemeteries at the turn of the nineteenth century. Today, markers appear to be reflections of corporate downsizing and efficiency rather than ornamental memorials to the deceased. Headstones lay flat into the ground, allowing for easier maintenance. These patterns enable students to understand past and present attitudes toward death.

Making the Activity Meaningful

In workshops, teachers often ask me why we should take our students on field trips when we have so much to cover and so little time to do it. I am fully aware of the dilemmas teachers face regarding not only field trips but a variety of extended activities that appear to take up valuable time. However, we need to ask ourselves if we are teaching just to cover the curriculum or if we are teaching to create both excitement and actual knowledge. Based on my own experience and the experiences of many colleagues, I believe that experience-based, or activity-based, education is the key to unlocking learning potential in young people. Dan Rea (1999) suggests the following strategies to make learning more meaningful to students. Each strategy is naturally embedded in cemetery activities.

Strategy 1: CURIOSITY. Teachers need to create curiosity by using novelty, variety, discrepancy, suspense, surprise, and mystery. Teachers can keep students stimulated and curious by using active teaching methods such as role plays, reenactments, simulations, field trips, group projects, reports, games, model constructions, and class discussions.

Strategy 2: CHALLENGE. Challenge students with thought-provoking questions and open-ended problems.

Strategy 3: CHOICE. Encourage student choice by allowing options and preferences.

Strategy 4: CREATIVITY. Allow students opportunities to explore, create, design, fantasize, and play with information.

These four suggestions are derived from John Dewey's experience-based curriculum (1916) and provide the philosophical basis for cemetery investigations.

Because experience itself is part of the process of adjustment to a changing environment, knowledge is defined in terms of the interaction with a problematic situation. Dewey divides this process into five steps: (1) suggestions leaping forward to a possible solution; (2) the isolation of a problem into a definite question; (3) the postulation of a tentative hypothesis; (4) the rehearsal in the imagination of various avenues of solution; and (5) the testing of the hypothesis by overt or imaginative action (41–53).

Dewey's five steps are employed as guidelines for students when performing their field observations and subsequent analysis in the classroom. I divided the activity into three stages: (1) students observe a fieldstone and I teach them Dewey's five steps, or what is commonly known as the scientific method; (2) students select their own carved stones; and (3) students perform an analysis of an entire family plot. Although the discovery of unusual stones generates a lot of enthusiasm, this activity can be adapted for students not able to access an actual site by using slides, photographs, or a series of grave rubbings.

Stage 1. Armed with notebooks, measuring tapes, and cameras, the class proceeds to the oldest section of the cemetery. It is preferable to locate headstones made from fieldstones that do not bear any inscriptions. Once the initial excitement has abated and students are seated around the stones, ask the following question: "What can one learn about the early social life of this community from these early grave markers?" Quite often the response is, "Nothing, these are just old rocks." Through direct observation and some gentle prodding from the teacher, students begin to talk about what they observe. They discuss the size of the stones as well as the material, the shape, and the placement. It is essential that they conduct their own observations. After they compile a list of observations, they formulate a number of tentative hypotheses. Several examples follow:

1. The use of old rocks rather than carved slate might mean that the early settlers were poor, illiterate, or running from hostile Native Americans.

2. The short distance between the head- and footstones seems to indicate that people were shorter then than they are today or that this is a burial ground for children.

3. All the stones are placed in the same direction, which might reveal something about the deceased's religious beliefs.

The student's list provides a basis for additional questions. Through the use of Dewey's method, a crude profile of early life in the colonies emerges. This profile is confirmed or rejected in the subsequent classroom discussion following the completion of the field experience.

Stage 2. Dewey's method is reinforced throughout stage 1 so that, at its conclusion, students are ready to select their own gravestones and present some tentative hypotheses regarding the history of the departed individuals buried under those stones. Each student presents his or her analysis with a photograph or a grave rubbing upon completion of this activity in the formal classroom. Soon, students can discover patterns that offer clues to their past. Twenty to thirty grave rubbings and photographs displayed in the classroom create a visual impact that gives students an appreciation of their own town's history.

Inscriptions on the stones contain enough information for students to derive explanations almost immediately. It is the task of the student to analyze this information to develop a hypothesis that more fully explains the circumstances surrounding the death. The two epitaphs in Figures 2–1 and 2–2 were taken from student-selected stones.

Readers may draw their own tentative hypotheses to explain the events surrounding the deaths of these two young people. These epitaphs easily transcend the social science curriculum and can be incorporated into writing and science activities. With a degree of historical insight and imagination, students can write short stories to help them think about history in a way that connects them to it. High levels of infant mortality suggest areas of investigation in health, nutrition, and the fertility patterns of the earliest settlers.

Stage 3. By this time, not only are students excited by their own investigations, but they also possess a sufficient degree of expertise in order to analyze an entire family plot, with the expectation that they will write a generational history. Here, the students trace births, marriages, deaths, and events over time. From the individual study in stage 1 to the generational analysis in stage 3, patterns are more clearly defined, and tentative explanations suggested in previous stages can be confirmed or rejected.

When all three stages are completed, a new world has opened to the students. Through their own observations and research, they have

Figure 2–1
Here Lyeth Buried Ye Body of William Button of Jersey.
Aged 37 Years. Died Ye 19 Day of October 1693.

learned about some of the lives of our country's earliest settlers. They can make generalizations as to infant mortality rates, multiple marriages, occupations, ethnicities, levels of wealth, and changing religious and social attitudes. In a sense, they have written their own history.

Activity: Cemetery Exploration

It would probably be helpful if students worked together in pairs.

1. Look around the cemetery. Observe the following:
   - Styles of gravestones:
     - Tablets—Vertical stones that average two to four inches in thickness and are placed directly in the ground with no bases used. Could be made of marble, limestone, or sandstone.

Figure 2–2
Otis S. Son of Langdon & Elizabeth S. Brown. Died Dec. 25, 1848.
Aged 9 mos. (A Christmas death.)

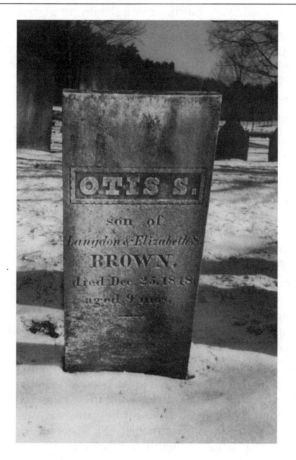

- Obelisk—Tall marker with a four-sided shaft of stone that is usually tapered and rises to a point. Usually made of marble.

- Slabs—Vertical stones that are placed vertically (upright) on a base and are six to eight inches in thickness. Often composed of granite.

- Crude stones—Small markers with no name or identifying marks of the person buried.

- Slates—Stone measuring the length of a person. Placed horizontally on the ground and bears an inscription.

- Placement of graves: Are they all facing the same direction? Do you think the direction they face is important?
- Boundaries of the cemetery: Is the cemetery marked by a fence, a sidewalk, paths, drives, shrubs, or in some other way?

2. Look at several family plots and choose one to study. Please make sure someone else has not already collected data from this plot. Write the following on an index card (put only one person on each card):

- Name of person—first, middle, and last name
- Gender
- Date of birth—year
- Date of death—year
- Age at death (calculate this if necessary)
- If available, information from gravestone that reveals cause of death. Do you think the individuals in the family plot are related or are husband and wife? How can you tell? Are other relatives buried in the same area? Are family burial areas more common in earlier graves or more recent graves?

3. Locate gravestones from different time periods that have epitaphs (written description, poem, verse, etc.). What do these epitaphs say? What might they reflect about attitudes toward death? How has the use of epitaphs and what epitaphs say changed over time? What might this mean?

4. Look at gravestones with men's names and gravestones with women's names from different time periods. How are men's and women's gravestones similar? How are they different? What might this tell you about the changing roles and statuses of men and women over time? (For instance, do the women's gravestones say, "Wife of . . ." as a way of identifying them?)

Expanded Curriculum. The value of this activity is that students are involved in a problematic situation, one that requires active participation. Gravestone analysis in a field setting also provides opportunities to expand the curriculum in a variety of ways.

1. Specific disciplines within the social sciences: Demographic patterns can reveal population patterns and ethnic diversity, which can be compared to regional and national movements. Students interested in economic issues can discern shifts as evidenced by type and quality of stones. Religious and social attitudinal changes have oc-

curred several times in our history and are manifested in gravestone inscriptions as well as in historic markers, which are discussed later.

2. Interdisciplinary investigations: Science and social studies offer exciting possibilities for studying the reasons for infant mortality and, conversely, longevity. Disease and epidemics can be investigated in terms of health and sanitation knowledge. The cyclical nature of fertility patterns prior to 1750 offers puzzles for the inquiring mind. Language arts can be employed to teach basic writing skills, to understand poetry and imagery among the earliest citizens, and to introduce literature written during that time. Writing a social history of a family based on gravestone analysis combines historical research and imagination, the kind of data on which historical novels are based. No study of cemeteries is complete without an understanding of the art form employed by the carvers. An investigation of medieval and Renaissance art is crucial to understanding the art forms inscribed on the earliest stones.

Dewey best sums it up when he states that "the inclination to learn from life itself [or in this case, death], and to make conditions of life such that students will learn in the process is the finest product of schooling" (1916, 41–53).

Things to Consider

Before taking my first class to the cemetery, I called the cemetery commission to obtain permission to bring my students there for historical research. The commissioner was delighted and welcomed the idea of using the cemetery to teach local history. He thought it was important to help young people understand their past, but he cautioned me about their behavior. Often, family members visit the graves of their relatives and they would be appalled to see young people running and jumping over the stones, he told me. Point well taken. A cemetery is a sacred place and our students need to learn how to conduct themselves respectfully when pursuing their cemetery research projects. A simple bit of advice for teachers planning field trips: A field trip is just another classroom, only the walls are farther away (see Chapter 10 for more advice on planning field trips).

A second very important issue is whether or not students can make grave rubbings as part of their project. A rubbing is created by carefully taping a piece of rice paper over the entire stone. The student then rubs the paper with a wax crayon. The result is a graven image. Since I first began requiring this activity, many local ordinances have prevented this practice because it defaces the stones over time. Today, I require students to photograph or sketch the inscriptions and fernery decorations on the stones. When we arrive in class after the trip, we have twenty-five to thirty images to analyze.

Historic Markers

Closely related to cemetery markers are historic markers, which are usually erected by a historical organization or a community to commemorate an event significant to the community or the nation. Kenneth E. Foote (1998) describes four ways in which communities designate events that are the tragic result of natural human violence and yet are worthy of remembrance. The first, sanctification, is a response that the community feels will result in creating or supporting a national identity. Foote cites Lincoln's dedication of the Gettysburg National Military Cemetery as a sanctified site as an example. Another example is the Andersonville National Historic Site, the only park in the National Park System to serve as a memorial to all American prisoners of war throughout the nation's history. In 1998, the National Prisoner of War Museum opened at Andersonville, dedicated to the men and women of this country who suffered captivity. Sanctified sites are clearly bounded from the immediate environment and marked with great specificity as to what happened. They are usually maintained for long periods of time and ownership typically transfers from private to public. These sites invite continual ritual commentaries and often attract additional and sometimes unrelated monuments and memorials (Foote 1998, 9). Sanctified sites clearly demonstrate a consensus among the community in terms of the values they represent. In both the Gettysburg and Andersonville sites, bravery and patriotism contribute to national identity.

A second response is designation. Somewhat less exalted than events that inspire sanctification, the events associated in designation "do not have the heroic or sacrificial qualities embodied in sanctified places" (17–18). The site of the Association of Martin Luther King Jr. at the Lorraine Motel in Memphis, Tennessee, was originally a designated site. Twenty years later, after a grassroots movement, King became viewed as a martyr in the civil rights struggle and the site became sanctified. Events reflecting minority struggles and labor difficulties are typically designated sites. The Lattimer Mine massacre in Pennsylvania, in which 19 miners were killed and 40 were wounded during a coal strike in 1897; the Triangle Shirtwaist fire in 1911, which claimed the lives of 146 young immigrant women; and the internment of Japanese Americans under Executive Order 9066 of February 19, 1942, to relocation centers from their homes in California are all examples of events that are commemorated with designated markers. Referring to historical memory as "storied places," Wallace Stegmen notes, "No place is a place until the things that have happened in it are remembered in history, ballads, yarns, legends, and monuments" (quoted in Glassberg, 7).

Monuments are visual reminders that denote particular places. "While psychologists connect sense of place to personal identity and recollection, cultural geographers and folklorists connect it to group communication and collective memory" (7). Monuments serve to identify a sense of place and at the same time maintain cultural continuity.

A third response is rectified sites. Usually, after a major event such as a fire or a shooting, this type of site resumes its original function. The great Chicago fire of 1871 and the less well known Peshtigo fire in Wisconsin, which occurred at the same time, are examples of events producing rectified sites. The Peshtigo fire destroyed twenty-four hundred square miles of timber and consumed the lives of eleven hundred individuals, making it the worst fire disaster in United States history at the time. As of this writing, the Los Alamos fire in New Mexico was raging, the result of a planned burn by the National Park Service gone awry. Though no lives have been lost, four hundred homes have been burned and a number of businesses disrupted. Tragic events like these do not create a sense of significance that inspires sanctification or designation. History is a litany of floods, fires, tornadoes, hurricanes, and accidents that have wrought devastation, interrupted lives, and in some cases changed the lives of communities, yet people return to rebuild their properties and resume their lives.

The final response, obliteration, is the way a community deals with something so horrendous it wants to bury it from memory. "In the words of Benedict Aderson, a shared history—elements of the past remembered in common as well as elements forgotten in common—is the crucial element in the creation of an 'imagined community' through which disparate individuals and groups can envision themselves as members of a collective with a common present and future" (Glassberg, 5). No markers designate the site; in fact, everything is done to obscure the site. Today, no one knows where nineteen Salem Villagers were hanged as a result of the 1690 witchcraft hysteria.

Analyzing Historic Markers

Historic markers become a gauge for interpreting how community attitudes are brought to bear on specific events. Very often, current perceptions of history influence the status a marker will receive. In their essay "Treaties and Memorials" (1996), Mary Ellen Cummings and Caroline Gebhard illustrate not only how a particular event becomes memorialized but, more important, how the interpretation of the event is presented. For example, until recently, the battle at Horseshoe Bend reflected a pro-Jacksonian position. Jackson defeated the Redsticks, moved on to the Battle of New Orleans, and defeated the British. He then became president of the United States, removed Native Americans from the East, and opened America to manifest destiny. The issue for local historians and national park curators today is whether Horseshoe Bend was a battle or a massacre. By his own account, Jackson reported losing twenty-six whites, eighteen Cherokees, and five Creeks in the battle, whereas eight hundred Redsticks including women and children were killed. This incident is an example of the many controversies that plague commemorative sites. "If our national memory, enshrined in parks like Horseshoe Bend, [is] to accord with these ideals, we must be willing to raise critical questions about how Native Americans are represented in public spaces, how our government reconstructs and retells its narrative of nation building, and how we might better include the voices of those who were forced to leave their homelands" (36).

In *Lies Across America* (1999), James W. Loewen examined hundreds of historical markers erected by local community organizations, church congregations, fraternity orders, and historic societies. With the exception of one marker erected in Bar Harbor, Maine, which read, "On this site in 1897 nothing happened," he found the markers he examined to be conspicuously negligent in accurately portraying the events they were commemorating. The greatest sin is omission. Part of the problem appears to be that marker committees or organizations tend to inscribe adulations based on their ideological perspectives or how they want history to be remembered. In my native state, New Hampshire, for example, a historic marker honoring Franklin Pierce, the only president from that state, stands in front of the Old North Cemetery in Concord.

Franklin Pierce 1804–1869

Fourteenth President of the United States (1853–57) lies buried in nearby Minot enclosure. Native son of New Hampshire, graduate of Bowdoin College, Lawyer, effective political leader, Congressman and U.S. Senator, Mexican War Veteran, courageous advocate of States Rights, he was popularly known as "Young Hickory of the Granite Hills."

Loewen (1999, 434–35) goes on to say that Pierce is presented to current generations as a "courageous advocate of States Rights." Contrary to being an advocate of states rights, however, Pierce adopted "a vigorous expansionist foreign policy" that was aimed at ridding the West of Spanish domination and opening new lands for Southern slave owners. His administration bungled the Ostend Manifest, which was designed to force Spain to sell Cuba, guaranteeing an expanded Southern slave empire. Pierce supported the Kansas-Nebraska Act, which opened Kansas to the possibility of slavery in 1854. In 1855, antislavery proponents met in Topeka to decide whether or not to allow slavery. Pierce refused to allow states rights and sent in U.S. dragoons to disperse the meeting. This act was soon followed by civil war in Kansas.

After Pierce left office, he endorsed Jefferson Davis for president. In 1863, when Vicksburg fell, he attacked the ideas of saving the Union. For the rest of his life, he was reviled and repudiated by New Hampshirites. National leaders of the 1850s have been described by some historians as the "blundering generation"; Pierce was perhaps the worst of the lot. And yet, in 1914, his statue was erected at the state capitol.

As a cautionary note, when we take students to visit historic sites, such as state and national parks that honor historic events, we cannot assume that the presentation will be balanced. Students should ask the following questions when visiting a site or completing an essay or report.

Ten Questions to Ask a Historic Site

1. When did this location become a historic site? (When was the marker or monument put up? Or the house "interpreted"?) How did that time differ from ours? From the time of the event or person commemorated?

2. Who sponsored it? Representing which participant group's point of view? What was their position in social structure when the event occurred? When the site went "up"?

3. What were sponsors' motives? What were their ideological needs and social purposes? What were their values?

4. Who is the intended audience for the site? What values were they trying to leave for us, today? What does the site ask us to go and do or think about?

5. Did the sponsors have government support? At what level? Who was ruling the government at the time? What ideological arguments were used to get the government to acquiesce?

6. Who is left out? What points of view go largely unheard? How would the story differ if a different group told it? Another political party? Race? Sex? Class? Religious group?

7. Are there problematic (insulting, degrading) words or symbols that would not be used today, or by other groups?

8. How is the site used today? Do traditional rituals continue to connect today's public to it? Or is it ignored? Why?

9. Is the presentation accurate? What actually happened? What historical sources tell of the event, people, or period commemorated at the site?

10. How does the site fit in with others that treat the same era? Or subject? What other people lived and events happened then but are not commemorated? Why? (Loewen 1999, 459)

In addition to using the preceding ten questions to analyze a historic site, some basic concepts in geography will help your students more fully understand historic sites. I have selected *Geography Standard 17: How to Apply Geography to Understand the Past to Illustrate How You Can Use*

Three of the Basic Themes of Geography (1986) to understand historic bat-tlefields. Though I have chosen to use the Battle of Manassas (Bull Run), the Union's first major defeat of the Civil War, for the following example, the same principles can be applied to most historic battles from the Battle of Bunker (Breeds) Hill to Custer's last stand.

Geography has influenced the rise and fall of empires. The defeat of the Spanish Armada in the English Channel due to a storm blowing out of the North Sea changed the fortunes of England and sent Spain into precipitous decline. Napoleon's army in 1812 and Hitler's Wehrmacht during WWII were defeated by the fury of Russia's winters. On June 6, 1944, General Eisenhower led the Allies in the largest land invasion in history, culminating in the defeat of Nazi Germany. The moon, tides, and the weather succeeded in creating opportunities for the Allies and surprise for the Nazis. Manassas, or the Battle of Bull Run, is another example of a military campaign that was influenced by geographic forces. Not only will the following model help your students under-stand one aspect of the Civil War, but it will demonstrate the funda-mental role geography plays in affecting events in history.

Activity: Using Historic Sites to Teach Geography—Manassas

On July 21,1861, a hot, sultry Sunday, Union and Confederate forces engaged in the first battle of the Civil War. In a sense it was a dress re-hearsal for what was to come. "By the close of the day, records and ac-tions would be shaping up names for the history books—Beauregard, Burnside, Jubal Early, Ewell, Hampton, A. P. Hill, Jackson, Longstreet, Sherman, Stuart, and many more—a bevy of 'greats' whose names would ring on the tongues of succeeding generations without respect to the side of which they fought" (Jones 1992, 4). Though the sides were equal in numbers—30,000 Union and 32,000 Confederates— only 18,000 of each saw action that day. By sunset, Confederate forces were able to rout the Union advance, not because of military tactics or superior firepower but because of a far greater advantage—geography.

Three geographic themes provide a prism to help students analyze the events at the Battle of Bull Run. These are location, place, and movement.

Location. First, I begin the lesson by asking students a series of ques-tions about location.

1. What is the absolute location of Manassas? Use an atlas to deter-mine the latitude and longitude of Manassas.

2. Where is Manassas located in relation to other important cities? Did it make a difference to the outcome of the battle?

3. What aspects of Manassas made it a good location for the first battle of the Civil War?

The following narrative provides the information necessary to analyze the concept of location.

Manassas is located approximately 39 N and 78 W, thirty miles from Washington City, the capital of the North, and ninety miles from Richmond, the capital of the Confederacy. On July 4, 1861, the United States Congress received a message from President Abraham Lincoln urging steps to save the Union. By July 16, Union forces had begun their march toward Manassas to control the rail line and proceed to Richmond. Meanwhile, in Richmond, General Robert E. Lee met with Jefferson Davis, president of the Confederacy. They viewed Bull Run as a site vital "for the protection of railroads at Manassas and possible offensive actions against the enemy" (Jones, 1992, 5).

In addition to protecting Manassas, Southern strategists devised other plans against the North. On July 14, 1861, Confederate General Pierre Gustave Toutant Beauregard sent the following communique to Richmond: "General Johnston currently commanding 12,000 men in the Shenandoah Valley should leave 3,000–5,000 men to check any Northern advance and move the remaining troops to reinforce Beauregard at Manassas Gap Railroad." The two of them planned to advance to Fairfax Court House, establish themselves between Union lines at Falls Church and Alexandria, attack them with a large force, drive them into the Potomac, and then attack Washington.

This plan did not materialize because Federal troops left Washington on July 16. By the 17th, they pushed on to the Fairfax Court House, ten miles from Washington, D.C., only to see Confederate troops in disorderly retreat. Federal troops advanced toward Manassas in large numbers and by the 18th commandeered the heights around the sleepy town of Centerville. Finding no resistance at Centerville, General Tyler took a squadron of cavalry and two light companies to make a reconnaissance—against instructions. He encountered Confederates encamped at Blackburn's Ford on Bull Run. Hidden by the cover of dense woods, the Southerners came alive "with volleys which showed that the whole bottom was filled with troops" (11). Tyler realized that the enemy was in force as his New York regiment fled in panic.

Place

For the discussion of place, I ask students the following question: What kind of place was Manassas before the battle took place? I want students to describe the physical and human characteristics based on their research. They need to provide information about what the people were like, including their attitudes and values. In addition, I provide a series of maps so students can determine to what extent rivers (runs), forests, open fields, and topography affected the battle. Again, the following narrative provides an analysis of place.

Place incorporates both the physical environment and the people who live in it or, in this case, the soldiers who participated in the battle. Bull Run is a narrow, crooked stream with marshy banks crossed by occasional fords and a stone bridge connecting one side of the Warrenton Turnpike to the other. Lee thought it a good place to protect the rail line and also a good staging area from which to attack Washington.

The country was deceptively pastoral. Gentle rolling hills were graced by large stands of deciduous trees and second-growth pine. Cleared fields spoke to the prosperity of the few scattered farms that covered the area. Henry Hill, where the crux of the battle took place, was only six miles from the rail junction at Manassas. In addition, several smaller runs, such as Cub and Rocky, flowed through it.

The men who fought in the Battle of Bull Run were remarkably similar. On the eve of the war, both the Union and the Confederate forces lacked training and discipline. General McDowell (Union) realized as he left Washington that his men were untrained and ill equipped. Captain Daniel P. Woodbury, U. S. Corps of Engineers, penned the following after the battle:

> An old soldier feels safe in the ranks, unsafe out of the ranks, and the greater the danger the more pertinaciously he clings to his place. The volunteer of three months never attains this instinct of discipline. Under danger, and even under mere excitement, he flies away from his ranks, and looks for safety in dispersion. At 4 o'clock in the afternoon of the 21st there were more than twelve thousand volunteers on the battle-field of Bull Run who had entirely lost their regimental organizations. They could no longer be handled as troops, for the officers and men were not together. Men and officers mingled together promiscuously; and it is worthy of remark that this organization did not result from defeat or fear, for up to 4 o'clock we had been uniformly successful. The instinct of discipline which keeps every many in his place had not been acquired. We cannot suppose that the troops of the enemy had attained a higher degree of discipline than our own, but they acted on the defensive, and were not equally exposed to disorganization. (National Historical Society 1985, 334)

A second problem for both armies was the confusion resulting from not being able to identify regiments. The uniforms of the day were a mosaic of colors and styles. Standard blue and gray uniforms had not been adopted. Each state sent volunteer outfits, each with different uniforms and colors. Two Zovares units, one from Louisiana and the other from New York, dressed virtually the same. Both units wore baggy

Turkish-style pants and the traditional red fez as a hat, copying the dress of French military units.

In the fog of battle, regiments were not identified soon enough. General Longstreet wrote this account: "The mistake of supposing Kirby Smith's and Elzey's approaching troops to be Union reinforcements from McDowell's right was caused by the resemblance, at a distance, of the original Confederate flag to the colors of the Federal regiments. This mishap caused the Confederates to cast about for a new ensign, brought out our battle flag, led to the adoption by General Beauregard, and afterwards by higher authority as the union shield of the Confederate's national flag" (56). On Henry Hill during the most horrific fighting, Major William Barry, Union commander, assured Captain Griffin that Stonewall Jackson's 33rd Virginia coming over the rise on Griffin's right was a regiment sent to support. Griffin's Parrott rifles, loaded with canisters, were prepared to fire. Uniforms worn by the advancing regiment gave no clue as to its loyalty. By the time the mistake was realized, the Southerners had advanced to within sixty yards of the Federals and opened fire. Fifty-four men and 104 horses were killed or wounded.

A final factor was the physical condition of the soldiers. Union forces had marched twenty miles from Washington to Centerville. Union intelligence proved to be inadequate. Instead of an additional six miles to Sudley Springs it was twelve miles as McDowell attempted to outflank Confederate forces with already-fatigued troops. By four o'clock in the afternoon, Union soldiers wearing sweat-soaked wool uniforms and fighting under a hot sun and oppressive humidity began to give up. Major Joseph P. Balch, First Regiment Rhode Island Volunteers, wrote, "In the retreat resulting from the turning of the right flank by our army by the enemy, the regiment was brought off in good order, with the brigade to which it was attached, without further serious casualty other than excessive fatigue arising from and natural to a march of some forty miles in fifteen to sixteen hours (400)."

The combination of fatigue and dehydration demoralized Union forces. On the other hand, General Johnston's Confederate reserves began arriving by rail from Winchester. This was the first time troops were transported by rail for a military engagement. As he fed his fresh units into battle at a critical time, the Union forces were overwhelmed and collapsed into disorderly retreat.

Movement

1. How did both the Union and the Confederate armies ship supplies to Manassas?

2. To what extent did delays in troop movements affect the outcome of the battle?

3. In what ways were movements impeded or advanced? Describe specific events during the battle that ultimately affected the result.

4. What other factors might have affected the outcome of the battle of Manassas?

The following narrative provides sufficient information to analyze the concept of movement.

Movement and its disruption were critical elements of the battle. Three events occurred that affected the outcome: (1) McDowell's delays in troop movements, (2) Evan's ability to hold Union forces at Stone Bridge, and (3) Johnston's use of Confederate troops by rail from Winchester. General Longstreet summarized the situation this way: "Johnston was sixty miles away from Beauregard, but the delay was three days, for McDowell's march via Sudley Springs, so reduced the distance in time and space as to make the consolidation easy under well organized transportation facilities" (National Historical Society 1985, 43).

On the night of the 20th, McDowell's intention was to move several columns down the Warrenton Turnpike so they would have a shorter march in the morning. Relying on poor advice from some of his officers, he waited to bring up reinforcements. Trouble for the Union march began early on the morning of the 21st. The artillery was on schedule, but the infantry was not. Originally, McDowell ordered Tyler's division to create a feint at Stone Bridge, leaving Hunter's and Heintzelman's divisions to turn right and arrive at Sudley Springs by 7:00 A.M. The earliest units arrived at 9:30 A.M., however. "At Sudley's Mill we lingered about an hour, to give men and horses water and a little rest before going into action," wrote Captain Daniel P. Woodbury (National Historical Society 1985, 333).

Meanwhile, a heavily fortified Confederate force delayed Tyler's division from crossing Stone Bridge. Assistant Adjutant General James B. Fry noted, "The enemy has planted a battery on the Warrenton turnpike to defend passage of Bull Run, has mined the Stone Bridge, and made a heavy abatis on the right bank to oppose our advance in that direction. The ford above the bridge is also guarded, whether with artillery or not is not positively known, but every indication favors the belief that he proposes defending the passage of the stream" (326).

Tyler's batteries commenced firing at 6:00 A.M. and were met with heavy resistance from Evan's batteries across the run. Evan held the Union forces in check until he realized that Hunter's and Heintzelman's troops had outflanked him. At about 8:30 A.M., he left four companies to guard the bridge and marched six companies to form a flank on Matthews Hill in order to frustrate the Union advance. "Union officer Fry later wrote in admiration, 'Evan's action was probably one of the best pieces of soldiership on either side during the campaign'" (Jones

Figure 2–3
Map #1 (Manassas #1).

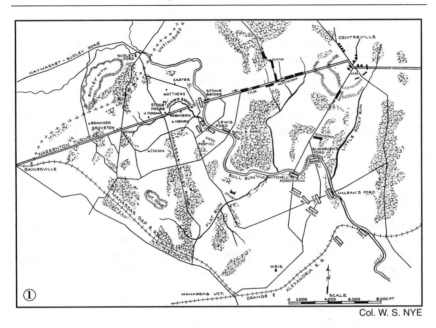

Col. W. S. NYE

1992, 27). At 9:15 A.M., the first of the Federals encountered Evan's fire. Hunter was wounded by a shell fragment, and by 9:45 A.M., Burnside had taken charge. He fought another hour against Evan's companies. As the Federal forces kept coming, Evans was forced to retreat but his gallantry had provided the Confederates what they desperately needed—time.

That element of time became the decisive factor in the battle late in the afternoon. Throughout the rest of the day the battle seesawed on Henry Hill. At almost sunset, General Johnston's fresh Confederates began arriving on the field. He used these units strategically and turned the tide on the battle for the Confederacy. The series of events during the day had finally caught up with the Union army. In disorderly rout, they returned to Washington, having been unable to achieve their first victory.

Though historians still debate what might have happened if the Union had won that first battle rather than the Confederacy, it is clear that the geographical context played a major role in affecting the outcome of the first battle of the Civil War at Manassas. The maps in Figures 2–3 and 2–4 further illustrate how geography affected that battle.

Analyze a Historic Site

Location

What is the absolute location of your historic site? Refer to atlases and maps to determine the latitude and longitude.

Where is your site in relation to major cities and towns? Did this make a difference?

What aspects of your site make it a good location? For settlement? For military advantage?

Place

What kind of place was your site before the historic event took place?

Describe its physical and human characteristics. Use topographical or aerial maps if possible. Did rivers, forests, plains, and so on affect the events in any significant way? What were the people like? Describe their attitudes and values.

Human-Environmental Interaction

How did humans change the environment at your historic site?

Did these changes affect human behavior in any way?

Movement

How were supplies shipped to your historic site?

In what way was movement impeded or enhanced? Describe rivers (frozen or free flowing), roads (muddy or dry), railroads (open or destroyed). What other obstacles might have affected the outcome of the events at your site?

Region

In what region of the country is your historic site located?

What climate does this region have? Consult climate maps. Did the time of the year influence the outcome of the events at your site?

Although these questions refer to Manassas they can be used to analyze any historic site or event.

Figure 2-4
Map #2 (Manassas #4).

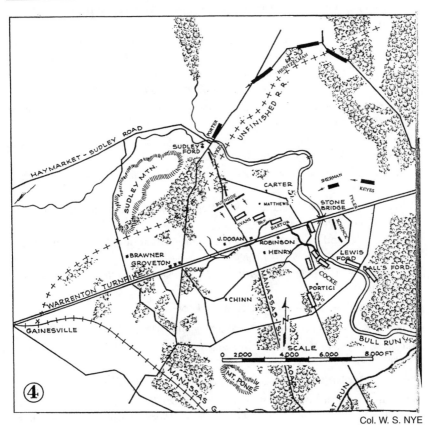

Col. W. S. NYE

References

Adams, N. 1875. *Annals of Portsmouth.*

Belknap, J. 1831. *The History of New Hampshire.* Vol. 1. Dover, NH: S. C. Stevens and Ela Wadleigh.

Conrad, J. A. 1989. *Developing Local History Programs in Community Libraries.* Chicago American Library Association.

Cummings, M. E., and C. Gebhard. 1996. "Treaties and Memorials: Interpreting Horseshoe Bend National Military Park." *The Public Historian* 18 (4).

Dewey, J. 1961 [1916]. *Democracy and Education* New York: McMillan.

Foote, K. E. 1998. *Shadowed Ground: America's Places of Tragedy and Violence.* Austin, TX: University of Texas Press.

Geographic Education Implementation Project. 1984. *7–12 Geography: Themes, Key Ideas, and Learning Opportunities.* Skokie, IL: Rand McNally.

Geography Education Standards Project. 1994. *Geography for Life: National Geography Standards.* Washington, D.C.: National Geographic Research and Exploration.

Hanson, E. 1824. *The Remarkable Captivity and Surprising Deliverance of Elizabeth Hanson.* 4th ed. Dover, NH.

Jenness, J. S. 1876. *Transcripts of Original Documents in the English Archives Relating to the Early History of the Study of New Hampshire.* New York.

Jones, A. 1992. *Civil War Command and Strategies: The Process of Victory and Defeat.* New York: Free.

Jones, V. C. 1992. *The Bull Run Campaign: First Manassas.* Eastern Acorn/Eastern National Park and Monument Association.

Kammen, C., ed. 1996. *The Pursuit of Local History: Readings on Theory and Practice.* Altermira.

Kidwell, C. S., and M. A. Plane. 1996. "Representing Native American History." *The Public Historian* 18 (4).

Konefes, J. L., and M. K. McGee. 1996. "Old Cemeteries, Arsenic, and Health Safety." *Cultural Resource Magazine* 10.

Loewen, J. W. 1995. *Lies My Teacher Told Me.* New York: Torchstone, Simms-Schuster.

———. 1999. *Lies Across America.* New York: New.

Longstreet, J. 1896. *From Manassas to Appomattox.* Dallas: Dallas Publishing.

Mahoney, J. 1981. *Local History: A Guide for Research and Writing.* Washington, D.C.: NEA.

May, R. 1926. *Early Portsmouth History.* Boston: C. E. Goodspeed.

National Historical Society. 1985. *The War of the Rebellion: A Completion of the Official Records of the Union and Confederate Armies.* Reprint. Historical Times.

Organization of American Historians. 1998. *American Stories: Collected Scholarship on Minority History.* Indiana University Printing Services.

Paulsen, G. 1996. *Hatchett.* New York: Aladdin.

Rea, D. 1999. "Serious Fun in Social Studies" Middle Level Learning Supplement, *Social Education.* (6) September.

Salstonstall, W. 1941. *Ports of Piscataqua.* Cambridge: Harvard University Press.

Turner, N. V. 1996. *Salzburgers Buried at Old Ebenezer Georgia 1734–1736.*

Wright, R. H., and W. B. Hughes III. 1996. *Lay Down Body: Living History of African-American Cemeteries.* Detroit: Visible Ink.

Special thanks to Commander William Cahill, U.S. Navy, retired, for the walks and insights at Manassas Battlefield.

Chapter Three

Write a History

A few days before I began teaching at Rye Junior High School in 1978, I met Mr. Wallace Smith, the history teacher I was about to replace, leaving the school. After many years of teaching, he had retired and was looking forward to moving to Sun City, Arizona. Like many good teachers, he had collected curriculum material, which he now offered to me. In the closet at the back of my new classroom, I found boxes full of history books, stacks of paper, maps, and record albums, all dating to the mid-1960s. Remember the old filmstrip projectors with audiocassettes? He had saved three boxes of those films, ranging from the Colonial experience to the Russian Revolution. One cold, rainy afternoon, I decided to sift through the closet, which reminded me of Merlin's warren, clear out what was not necessary, and organize the rest. To my surprise, I found several eighth-grade histories of Rye neatly stacked at the back of the closet. His students had written local histories of their community. The table of contents of one paper revealed that each student was assigned a topic to research and write. Their collective effort produced a student version of From Sandy Beach to the Present. What a great idea! I thought to myself. Today, this would be an excellent cooperative group activity.

Instead of requiring my students to write a local history, I taught them to write history essays using the standard five-paragraph format: introduction (1 paragraph), main body (3 paragraphs), and conclusion (1 paragraph). My students soon realized that an essay was due every Friday, regardless of weather. I wanted them to get plenty of writing practice. Then, each spring, they competed in the Daughters of the American Revolution essay contest. As you know, contests of this type are extremely time-consuming. That's why I selected only one for my students to participate in. Social Science Fair, National Geography Bee,

History Day, and Voice of Democracy are all excellent opportunities to help students learn to research, organize, and present history projects. I found the DAR contest was a good opportunity to teach the elements of lively writing. And the students responded positively: for seven years, students of mine won first, second, and third places at the regional level in Exeter, New Hampshire.

This chapter, which is based on that experience, addresses three questions: (1) What topics should grades 6–12 students include in a local history?, (2) How should students conduct historical research?, and (3) What strategies help students learn the elements of good writing? Daniel Webster once said, "It is wise to recur to the history of our ancestors. Those who do not look upon themselves as a link connecting the past with the future do not perform their duty to the world." Writing a local history will help students view themselves as a link between the past and the future. They get excited when they feel a connection to the past. Researching events that took place on a street they recognize, in a building they know, (however dilapidated), near a canal or a wharf they can walk along, or in a field or a meadow they can visit will enable them to touch history. Every town and city has a vivid history. Help your students learn about theirs.

Select a Topic

Let students select their specific topics for investigating local history. They need to feel an investment in their project. Usually, students will ask for assistance in identifying a topic for research. After all, at this point, they know very little. Two possibilities will guide them toward selecting their own topics: NCSS Standard III (1994) and a list of possible topics.

In 1994, the National Council for the Social Studies adopted the Curriculum Standards for the Social Studies. Standard III, People, Places, and Environments, suggests a series of research questions students can use as possible topics. The concepts of location, place, human-environmental interaction, and movement provide an excellent framework for investigating local communities.

Location

Why did Native American and early European explorers settle where they did? Locations along riverbanks, in the lee of forests, near game, and close to harbors all met the settlers' basic needs for water, food, shelter, and transportation. Which of these conditions were responsible for the history of your community?

Place

What kind of place was your community in 1600? In 1750? In 1900? Today? Students enjoy investigating old maps, looking at photographs, reading diaries and journals, and consulting local histories to aid them in writing their history papers. What geographical features gave rise to cultural attributes? What is the relationship between ethnic background, climate, and architecture? In the same way that hogans, wickiups, adobes, and tepees reflect materials available in particular environments, the saltbox house of New England, the half-timbered house in Pennsylvania, and the plantation style in the South reflect both the cultural backgrounds of the builders and the materials available. A sense of place affords grades 6–12 student researchers an opportunity to investigate the rich diversity of the many cultures that came into contact when the Old and New Worlds collided. Every history should explore early contacts between Native Americans and early settlers and contacts between succeeding waves of immigrants. What kind of place was their community, and how did it change?

Human-Environmental Interaction

Conflicts among cultures clearly emerge when students investigate patterns of land use. The use and/or abuse of land creates many difficult questions for students. Obviously, European expansion was inevitable, but what happens to the environment when large populations spill into new areas? How are food and shelter obtained? What are the consequences to the environment? As students wrestle with these questions, have them also consider what our relationship is to contemporary problems. Is the ecological sensitivity of earlier Native Americans helping us solve today's problems? To what extent should citizens respect nature or continue to try to control it for societal needs? As middle and high schoolers delve into a study of the expansion and the development of their community, what patterns can they detect? Which of these patterns are helpful or harmful? Some communities developed in a haphazard manner; others did not. What historical forces explain these differences? As students' historical investigation blends into the present, what trends can they predict for their community in the next twenty-five or thirty years?

Movement

America is a country on the move. It has a unique history of movement. How did the early settlers move to your community? Did they walk, sail on boats or barges, arrive in ox carts, ride on horseback, ride

in a train, or fly on a plane? Was your community a transportation center or a jumping-off point for further expansion? Did it decline because
it missed the rail line?

Movement examines tragedy and promise, from the Trail of Tears
to the gold rush. Look at social movement as well as physical movement. Do the rags-to-riches stories of Horatio Alger represent successful individuals in your community? Is it still possible for an ordinary
person to become president? Students investigating their communities
will continue to uncover the genius of inventors, politicians, and en-
trepreneurs that led to great wealth and power for some and tumbling
fortunes for others. What events contributed to the rise and fall of local citizens? To what extent are students immune from social dislocation? Does researching and writing about local history help them with
that question?

You can support these broad categories by discussing the following
specific topics with your students, which will illuminate even more
possibilities for them.

In the process of selecting a list of topics with your class, think
about the following questions and ideas. Concentrate on those that apply to your community. What events or time periods made history in
your town? For many, prerevolutionary history is fascinating. The early
settlers forged their way into the wilderness, endured physical hardships, and defended themselves against the Native Americans' attacks
during the French and Indian Wars. These were the frontier settlements,
and their contributions set the groundwork for a new social order.

During the Colonial period, as society became prosperous, other
towns and cities dominated the social and political events of the time.
The larger seaboard communities, with their maritime industries, were
influential during the American Revolution. Visits by Washington and
Lafayette indicated their importance.

As the economy changed, its influence was felt. Towns and cities
famous during the American Revolution were eclipsed by burgeoning
cities of the Industrial Revolution. The rapid demographic changes in
America pushed many immigrants into industrial cities, as well as forc-
ing many out and westward to the new frontier.

Early Origins

What conditions led to the founding of your town or city, and are those
influences still felt? The first settlements were located near water, either
on the ocean or along rivers flowing to the sea. Fishing and lumbering
were the primary industries. In many New England communities, the
church was not only the ecclesiastical authority but also the civil authority. Many early towns were founded because the inhabitants did

not want to walk great distances to Sunday services. Theocracies developed and remained until the early 1800s.

Other cities, such as Lowell, Lawrence, and Holyoke, Massachusetts, and Nashua and Manchester, New Hampshire, were clearly industrial cities. At the height of economic activity, the Amoskeag Mills in Manchester produced fifty miles of fabric a day. Towns along the Ohio and Mississippi Rivers were jumping-off points for westward expansion. Carl Sandburg's Chicago and Andrew Carnegie's Pittsburgh reflected the enormous economic development of the cattle and steel industries. The immigrants squeezed into the cities, their backgrounds and cultures in their baggage, giving America its distinctive ethnic qualities. Their contribution to local history needs to be recorded.

The expansion of the railroad, particularly after the Civil War, fueled the growth of cities. From manufacturing to distribution, the rails carried products across America. Great rail centers sprang up, and with them, a city's history. When the golden spike connected east with west, our culture and that of the Native American experienced profound changes.

Economy

Cities and towns rise and fall with the economy. What happened in your community during times of recession and depression? What happened when a new technology was invented? Did your town prosper or decline? How were the lives of residents affected by economic changes? Investigate the ebb and flow of economic forces as you select your topics. Is it an appropriate area of study for your local history?

With these broad ideas in mind, what specific topics can be investigated in writing a local history? A cursory view of a table of contents of any local history will provide a chronology for students to follow. However, particular towns have topics peculiar to their history. The next section will represent a scattering of specific topics to consider as you continue to plan a local history.

A history of a local community is a history of the lives of a people. Knowing how they lived and what they did provides insight into the ordinary circumstances of life for most people. A study of the social history of a community reveals the reasons for its customs, habits, and mores.

Amusement and Sports

Many games and sports played in Colonial America are seldom heard about today. Sports not only tell what people did in leisure time but also what values the society supported. In Lancaster, New Hampshire, two political occasions—the annual regimental muster and the semiannual terms of the highest court in May and November—prompted games on a local level. People thronged the streets to watch parades and filled the fields to participate in games. Wrestling was a big sport, inviting competition among towns. Lancaster citizens also enjoyed swimming, including diving off the "spring board" into the flume above the sawmill; pitching "quates" (quoits); and rolling tenpins. On the Fourth of July, the townspeople made "fireballs," a domestic product made of a long candlewick and a ball of string soaked in turpentine. "The rapidity of handling prevented burning hands, and deft players would soon have the air alive with fiery arcs, tangents, parabolas, and, as the balls burned out, blazing stars of fragments" (Stanley 1987, 353).

Weather

Prior to urbanization, most people were dependent on the weather for survival. An early frost could ruin their harvest, storms destroyed valuable property, and lightning burned barns full of hay. In Barnstead, New Hampshire, the summer of 1769 was called "the cold summer." "Frosts were seen in every month of the year. The year after the 'cold summer,' winter came in intensely cold and remained with very deep snows for forty days in succession" (Jewett 1872, 189). The year 1815 was no delight and was memorable for its deep snows. The woods were filled with eight feet of snow, and, as late as May 19, nine inches fell. A snowy spring was followed by a tempestuous fall. On September 23, the greatest gale ever recorded struck, blowing down much of the primeval forests. Students can imagine what effects weather had on earlier settlers and how the lives of settlers were shaped by natural forces.

Early Schools and Education

Investigating the history of schools in a local community is yet another way to understand our heritage. In 1647, the Central Court of Massachusetts passed an act that was the basis for public education in the Bay Colony and influenced the establishment of a public school system in the other New England colonies as well. The act required that towns of fifty households or more provide instruction in reading and writing and went on to suggest possible ways of financing such a system. From that time forward, schools and education reflected local community attitudes and values.

"In Newfields, New Hampshire, the early schools were located in private homes, and, not infrequently, barns were used as school rooms" (Fitts 1912, 328). A school in Canterbury, New Hampshire, exhibited similar problems. "Tradition has it that these school rooms were not always the best the house afforded, one being located, it is said, so near to a hog pen that the grunting of the animals frequently disturbed the teacher and pupils" (Lyford 1912, 378).

In most of the colonies, schools were different for boys than for girls. Apprentice programs for the boys and dame schools for the girls existed, as well as Latin schools and academies. Yet, in New Hampshire, equal opportunity was the hallmark of education. "In marked contrast with the people of other New England colonies, the settlers of New Hampshire very early made provisions for the coeducation of the sexes" (Lyford 1912, 385). Lyford goes on to cite that Hampton in 1649, Dover in 1658, and Portsmouth in 1773 provided for the education of all children who were capable of learning to read, write, and cast accounts.

Students enjoy investigating how early schools were organized, run, and maintained. Let them write a history essay or a section of their local histories about the schools in their community, the curriculum used, the types of teachers employed and their training, and, of course, discipline procedures.

Accidents and Casualties

Calamities, accidents, and casualties that befell people in earlier times are other areas worthy of research. Students' imaginations are captured when they read accounts of accidents in early newspapers and local histories. Small children were frequently scalded by or drowned in buckets of water. Older people were kicked by horses or run over by carriages. They fell out of trees or trees fell on them. Drownings occurred as regularly as rain, and several accounts of self-inflicted gunshot wounds pepper the pages of local histories.

In Cornish, New Hampshire, two reported accidents testify to the agricultural nature of society. "In 1858, Arthur Wyman, age thirteen, son of Milton Wyman was sliding in a field near his school house, when his sled struck a pile of frozen manure, breaking it, and a port of it was driven into his body several inches. From the effects of this he died after a few hours of extreme suffering." And from the same account, in 1870: "8-year-old Willie Chase was playing in a barnyard and was accidentally hit in the head by a piece of frozen manure, which caused his death" (Childs 1910, 198).

Two other bizarre accidents involving school-age children occurred in New Hampshire. On a tombstone in Rye, the following epitaph is inscribed, "Sheridan, Son of Jonathan Philbrick, Esq. & Sarah, His Wife, Was Instantly Killed by Lightening, While at School, June 30, 1824, Aged 11 years." The *History of the Town of Peterborough, NH* reports, "On June 23, 1838, Hannah Jane, daughter of John Chapman, killed by a window sash falling upon her neck in her attempt to get into a school-house in Jaffrey. The blocking under her feet fell falling away and leaving her hung by the neck, age twelve years, five months" (237).

How to Research Local History

What sources should students use and why? Two basic types should be distinguished—*primary* sources (original documents) and *secondary* sources (interpretive sources). Students investigating their local community can usually find primary sources at the local historical association, the public library (in the special collections section), local churches, and municipal offices. Reading original documents, records, and maps engages the students' interest and, at the same time, provides an authentic experience since they are using the materials professional historians use. Students who research New England records will find an abundance of material. "For the first New Englanders, then, Puritanism and the fear of the uncivilizing ways of the wilderness account in considerable measure for the amazing proliferation of records at every level of society. This penchant for recording events in public and private life distinguishes the Colonial New Englander from his counterpart in the mid-Atlantic and southern colonies" (Crandall 1984, 8). Secondary sources and interpretive histories should also be consulted to place local events in a broader social and historical context. Teach students how to use the following sources for their research.

Newspapers

Students should learn to read newspapers with a critical eye. The information they contain is useful, but newspapers were business enterprises, not historical journals. Profit was the primary motive. However, in spite of those concerns, newspapers do furnish valuable local information. Most libraries keep microfiche copies of local editions as well as national editions. Student researchers can copy them and then study them at home or in the classroom.

Personal Diaries and Journals

Historical societies and special collections sections of the public library house diaries, journals, and personal manuscripts. Some entries provide anecdotal accounts, others offer specific information, particularly if business was transacted, and a few reveal the authors' reflections about their time period. Although bias is a consideration, often these accounts are the only materials that can provide an understanding of events from a personal perspective.

Records

Municipal, state, federal, organizational, and church records provide information that helps students understand local events. Tax records, street directories, vital statistics (births, deaths, and marriages), and school records can be easily obtained through public libraries and municipal offices. Students' interest is charged when they read documents and records in their original form.

Maps

Villages became towns, and towns became cities. Early maps reveal the original roads, boundaries, and houses in a community. Locations of businesses such as wharfs, gristmills, sawmills, factories, and rail depots are identified. When students compare early maps to more recent maps of their community, they can ascertain demographic changes.

Photographs

The camera's eye allows students to see what their community was like in previous generations. They are often surprised to see the many changes that have occurred. Trees no longer stand where they once did, buildings have been replaced by shopping malls, condominium complexes have arisen in former meadows, and in some communities, gentrification has replaced old neighborhoods. By focusing on business names painted on storefronts, horse-drawn wagons, hoopskirted women, laborers building by hand, and boys lazily fishing, early photographers captured for today's students a historical picture of their community. Students can determine from photographs not only facts about their community but also what is missing in the pictures, leading to further inquiry.

Throughout the process of researching local history, students have an obligation to strive for accuracy. The necessity of taking careful notes cannot be overemphasized. Once the process of research is completed, the next step is to write the results in an exciting way that creates interest for the reader.

How to Write Local History

Unless you teach in a school that has embraced a writing-across-the-curriculum program, you will probably encounter students who are reluctant to write in a social studies or history class. Sixth graders are no different than seniors. After all, they'll say, isn't writing supposed to be taught in an English or a language arts class? I spent many years teaching social studies through writing. This section will introduce you to some strategies I found successful. If you decide to engage your students in writing a local history, the following steps will be helpful.

Students will need three-by-five-inch index cards or a loose-leaf notebook for jotting down notes or quotes. On their cards they will document sources with book title and page number. Some will need a special notebook or box, because they will need to organize their data. Because most libraries now have copy machines, rolls of dimes and quarters are in order if copying is going to replace note taking.

Once the material has been gathered, students will need to organize it. The standard outline format is all they need to use. All the information must relate to the topic selected. If it doesn't, they should throw it away. In his or her paper, the student must state the intention, tell the teacher what will be learned, and explain why it is important. Simply stated, the paper must have an introduction, a main body, and a conclusion.

Write the First Draft Using the Five Senses

If history is to come alive and connect in some way to students, it must be smelled, touched, seen, heard, and tasted. They should be encouraged to use five sense descriptions per handwritten page. Not only will this create interest for the reader, but it will help students feel what it must have been like to live in a different era. Sense descriptions must fit into a historical period; for example, George Washington never heard Martha's voice over a phone line.

> Smell: The sweet fragrance of apples baking in the kitchen fireplace, bubbling and spitting the newly bought cinnamon, blended with the aroma of freshly poured cream.

> Touch: Rachel spread the down-filled quilt, soft as newly hatched chicks in spring, over her brother's trundle bed.

> Sight: Sunlight streamed across the fresh-mowed meadow. The pewter pitcher cast a long shadow from the softly lit taper placed at the end of the well-scrubbed table.

> Sound: Clanging bells interrupted the termagant squabbling of barn swallows, inviting the congregation to Sunday's service. Wagons bumped and clattered over the corduroy road.

> Taste: Simon savored the vinegar and molasses switchel as he continued to cut hay with his uncle's scythe.

As students use sense descriptions, they will naturally fall into imagery, metaphors, and similes. Once again, the metaphor must fit the situation. "The Mexican landscape was as flat as a tortilla" is better than "the Mexican landscape was as flat as a pancake."

You may want to read some examples of good descriptive writing to your students. Thomas Wolfe describes autumn in Maine with its frost "sharp and quick as driven nails," its blazing, bitter red maples, and other leaves "yellow like a living light . . . falling about you like small pieces of sun" (1961, 177). "Near the trees were thousands of tents and canvas-roofed huts, and across the fields and hills were neither tents nor trees but mile upon mile of trenches, scarring the earth with grotesque irregular patterns, the ground between them bristling with tangles of abatis and sinister sharpened stakes of chevaux-de-frise," writes Bruce Catton, describing the encampments on the outskirts of Petersburgh during the Civil War (2001, 319).

Critique and Rewrite

When the rough or working draft is in process, students should read sections to the class for criticism. Students need to learn how to critique the work of others as well as how to accept criticism. It is up to the teacher to set up the conditions for this process. The critique should be a positive process aimed at improving the quality of each student's essay. The teacher, as editor, must show enthusiasm, discuss a good idea, and then have the student think about a better way to express it, at all times using positive reinforcement. Students who offer comments must be reminded to be courteous and sensitive to others' feelings. Students may critique by presenting positive comments first and then offering one helpful suggestion. The critique forum is a place where students should be assisted in generating new ideas, checking for historical accuracy, reconsidering what they have written, and rewriting to improve their essays.

Revision for students is somewhat different from what it would be for a mature writer. The first draft, by definition, is exploratory; it omits material and most often does not have a strong introduction or conclusion. However, it does provide a structure from which to add, delete, and change the order of information. In some instances, the student may decide to scrap the topic and select a new one. The most difficult task for students is to accept the idea that completing several revisions is fundamental to good writing. Bruce Catton, the highly successful Civil War historian, admitted to constant revision of his work. Class time and homework time should be set aside for student revision with specific objectives, such as rewriting using active voice only, checking for historical accuracy, or taking what they have written and cutting the number of words in half. This works, but be prepared for a maelstrom on your first attempt. At least three formal teaching periods should be devoted to writing the introduction, the main body, and the conclusion. Other periods can be used for peer review in small groups, individual writing, and general discussion.

A good introduction grabs the reader immediately. Getting students to write and orally present grabbers and "gotcha" sentences is time well spent. Almost any American will tell you that the American Revolution started in Lexington and Concord with the shot heard round the world, yet the fact is that the first hostilities against the Crown took place at Fort William and Mary in New Castle, New Hampshire, on December 13 and 14, 1774, after Paul Revere rode to Portsmouth, New Hampshire, to warn the Committee of Safety of General Gage's intentions.

Unknown facts, twists of fate, ironies, and unusual situations constantly turn up when researching local history. Use them to help students develop grabbers. John Paul Jones was a cabin boy at the age of twelve and commanded his first ship at age sixteen. The average woman spinning wool "walked" twenty miles a day in front of the spinning wheel. Grabbers are developed from facts such as these.

Once he has written the introduction to capture the reader's attention, the writer must continue to hook or pull the reader along with a series of well-developed paragraphs, which form the main body of the paper. Each subtopic heading from the outline is a new paragraph or aspect that further develops the central idea, or thesis. Several related facts support each new idea. An essay can be conceived like a mobile, geometrical and balanced:

Main Idea
Grabber

Subtopic   Subtopic   Subtopic
Fact   Fact   Fact   Fact   Fact   Fact   Fact   Fact   Fact

Conclusion

Which subtopic comes first? That depends on how the writer chooses to present the material. Historical events can be presented chronologically, year by year. Or a student can describe a series of incidents that lead to an outcome that is followed by consequences. In the case of a historical figure, one can begin at birth and recount significant experiences culminating in the action(s) that made the person famous. However, as Bates said, "The chronological method is almost always the best way to write history or biography and is almost essential for explaining a process in which time relationships play an important role" (1978, 67).

The most difficult paragraph for students to write is the conclusion. Some writers argue that the conclusion should come no later than the second paragraph of the essay itself; others say it should appear at the end. What can a young writer do? Develop a sentence that draws a relationship between the central idea of the essay and a modern problem or consequence: "As a result of the terrible losses suffered at Pearl Harbor, the United States today spends billions of dollars on national defense." Showing a relationship between the past and the present helps students understand that the present is an extension of the past and that events do not take place in a vacuum. But more important, the students have drawn that relationship. In a sense, they are historians.

References

Bates, J. D. 1978. *Writing with Precision*. Washington, D.C.: Acropolis.

Catton, B. 2001. *This Hallowed Ground: The Story of the Union Side of the Civil War*. Wordsworth Military Library.

Childs, W. H. 1910. *History of the Town of Cornish*. Vol I. Concord, NH: Rumford.

Cogswell, the Rev. E. C. 1878. *History of Nottingham, Deerfield and Northwood*. Manchester, NH: John B. Clarke.

Crandall, R. J. 1984. *Genealogical Research in New England*. Baltimore: Genealogical Publishing.

Edwards, N., and H. G. Richey. 1963. *The School in the American Social Order*. Boston: Houghton Mifflin.

Fitts, the Rev. J. H. 1912. *History of Newfields, NH*. Concord, NH.

Jewett, J. P. 1872. *History of Barnstead*. Lowell, MA: Marden and Rowell.

Lyford, J. O. 1912. *History of Canterbury, NH, 1727–1912*. Concord, NH: Rumford.

Parsons, L. B. 1905. *History of Rye, NH, 1623–1903*. Concord, NH: Rumford.

Stanley, J. C. 1987. "Local Schools: Exploring Their History." *History New Hampshire* 42 (4): 353.

Wolfe, T. 1961. "No Door." In *The Short Novels of Thomas Wolfe*, ed. H. C. Holman. New York: Charles Scribner's Sons.

Young, H. E. 1953. *History of Pittsfield, New Hampshire*. Concord: New Hampshire Bindery.

Chapter Four

The American House

We are what we build. From the original settlements along the eastern seaboard to the latest housing tracts encroaching on farmlands and open spaces, our values are embedded in our structures. To better understand local history, middle and secondary school students need to examine the history of architectural styles and housing patterns in their own communities. Too often we pass old buildings and do not understand what we see. "Formal instruction in learning to look at objects can be a major strategy for teaching students to select, discriminate, analyze, categorize, and synthesize," in order to help them understand their natural and man-made environments, Terry Zeller reminds us (1984, 57). This chapter will suggest activities for helping students understand architectural and housing patterns in their local communities.

Builders in the colonies were true to the heritage they left behind. They tended to re-create, as faithfully as circumstances permitted, the style of buildings in their former communities rather than invent new styles. The conforming cottages of the early English settlements in New England were remarkably similar to the villages along England's southwest coast. Germans in Pennsylvania, unlike their English counterparts who settled along the inland waterways, instead "followed the trail of limestone soil where the tall trees flourished and good farming awaited only the clearing of land" (Smith 1976, 127). Half-timbered houses in the traditional style of Rhineland medieval communities were reproduced on the rich soil of the Pennsylvania farmlands.

The American house became an expression born of utilitarian necessity and elegant refinement—sturdy in structure and gracious in simplicity. Immigrants adapted European styles to local conditions;

climate and building materials, including lumber and an endless variety of stone, contributed to unique style of house built on the edge of the frontier. The result was a rectangular structure that was similar throughout the colonies and yet at the same time reflected the distinctive qualities of each geographical region. Between 1620 and 1900, six basic styles evolved: Medieval, Colonial, Georgian, Federal, Greek Revival, and Victorian.

Medieval 1620–1675

The earliest cottages built along the eastern seaboard were replicas of buildings found in England and Holland. Builders employed the wattle and daub method. They wove twigs in a frame and smeared it with mud to form a wall. A steep-pitched thatched roof with a hole for smoke sat above the walls. Because of the heavy snows and rains in New England, and the rain and humidity in the Southern colonies, this style soon proved impractical. The structures experienced extremes in weather that made their wattle shrink and swell and eventually crack. In New England at this time, a log cabin—which might have solved their housing problems—was unheard of. One structure the colonists had experimented with—a stockade of sharpened logs filled with mud—had proved unsuccessful. "Therefore, New Englanders directed their energies toward perfecting and expanding the woodframe, clapboard sheathed cottage. It was their solution to the problem of shelter in their new environment" (Elliot and Wallas 1977). (See Figure 4–1.)

Colonial 1650–1700

The Colonial house was not one particular style but fell into several categories determined by local geography and the background of the builder. New England had a distinctive style different from that of the Southern colonies, and the style of the Dutch middle colonies differed from both. However, in spite of individual variation, all of these early houses shared some elements in common. Each house began with one room with a fireplace at one end, soon followed by the addition of a second room. Whole or partial cellars, usually made of stone, were dug. Ridge roofs were erected without dormers. All of these houses were built using a post-and-beam method. Large posts held up even larger horizontal timbers to complete the frame. All intersections were joined with a particular joint and tenoned together. No nails were necessary. The original planks that covered the frame could be made from clapboards or shakes and were plastered on the inside.

Figure 4–1
Sherburne House, Strawbery Banke Museum,
Portsmouth, NH, Late 17th Century

Figure 4–2
Restored Center-Chimney Colonial, Rye, NH.

From about 1675, these houses evolved to include one-and-one-half-and two-story Colonials one room deep and the central-hall Colonial with two rooms front and back. The facade reflected the location of the house and the skill of local craftsmen. The Colonial best represented the newly emerging social order—unified in its basic structure, yet diverse in details and refinements. (See Figure 4–2.)

Georgian 1720–1810

Georgian houses began to appear as early as 1720. They represented the English influence of King George and the growing prosperity of the colonies. Two major features dominated this architectural style: (1) a change in chimney location from the single center chimney of the earlier Colonial to two chimneys, one on each end of the house and (2) the emergence of a central hall and the use of fine architectural details.

> The facades were given an air of importance and solidity by replacing corner boards with pilasters and quoins; the roofs finished off with box cornices trimmed with moldings and supported by dentils. Inside, the doors and windows of these houses were made elegant with applied moldings, and the rooms finished with picture moldings and cornice moldings. (Williams and Williams 1957, 74)

One must realize that differences occurred between the early and later Georgian styles and between the style of the Southern and Northern Georgian structures. As the Federal style developed, a more detailed form of Georgian evolved. (See Figure 4–3.)

Federal 1810–1830

The American Revolution sparked a change, not only in relations with the Mother Country but also in architecture. Departing from English influence, the Federal style was a more austere form of Georgian. Stripped of its robust ornamentation, the style was severely classical. Detail became more important. More elegant ornamentation and also more delicacy and refinement punctuated the Federal style.

For the untrained eye, it is difficult to draw distinctions between the late Georgian and Federal styles. However, a few differences in detail reveal the line of demarcation. Federal style employed flush boarding, painted brick, or stucco to create the sense of compact solidity. Elliptical fanlights were placed in doorways. The interiors aimed at more functional use of space by incorporating curved walls, alcoves, elliptical rooms, and rounded corners. The effects were a more interesting interior, increased options for furniture arrangement, and a more pleasant living space.

Figure 4–3
Macpheadris-Warner House, Portsmouth, NH (1723).

Greek Revival 1820–1840

The breakaway from the rigid floor plan and simplicity of the Colonial led to the development of the Greek Revival style. After the American Revolution, the Georgian style lost its vitality and the newly formed nation demanded a new architecture. The democratic foundations of the new society provided the inspiration for the classical Greek form of architecture. It has often been called the architecture with white pillars, though it ranges from the look of an ancient Greek temple to that of a square Colonial with a massive square-posted porch over the front door.

The dominant characteristics of Greek Revival include the use of pillared porticos and pediments, a low, almost flat roof, suppression of chimneys, and impressive doorways. Greek architecture was intended to be made of stone, as many buildings were, particularly public ones. But many beautiful buildings were constructed of wood, as availability of local lumber and resources dictated.

Victorian 1836–1900

The advent of the Industrial Revolution changed housing in America in profound ways, as evidenced by the Victorian style. The Victorian house, sometimes called a gingerbread house or a wedding cake house, was substantially different from its predecessors in several ways. Mass production was responsible for a new concept of building called balloon framing, a method that employed two-by-four stud walls, thus eliminating post-and-beam framing. Central heating systems gave rise to more efficient stoves. The massive chimneys housing many fireplaces were reduced to accommodate only flues. Rooms were made larger and extended out into bay windows and other projections, and ceilings became higher, establishing a sense of spaciousness. Labor-saving devices replaced the skilled housewrights of previous generations.

Several offshoots of the Victorian developed, all basically Medieval Gothic in style. Materials were becoming cheaper, enabling more individuals to build homes, and limitations once imposed on builders because of design were lifted, creating great variety within this time period. Piazzas, wooden icicles on fretwork supported by brackets, and stained glass, not to mention turrets, were all building trends of the Victorian period.

Figures 4–4 through 4–6 show examples of floor plans from the Medieval period through the Georgian. They are an attempt only to

---

Figure 4–4

#1 Original two room dwelling

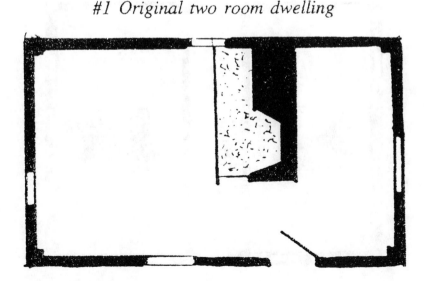

Figure 4–5

#2 Center Chimney Colonial

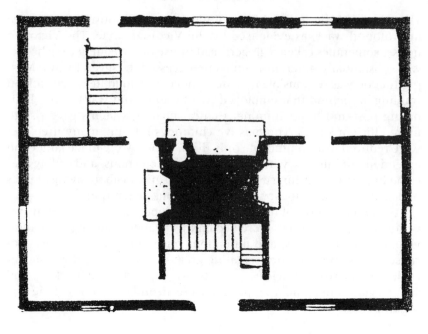

Figure 4–6

#3 Central Hallway Georgian

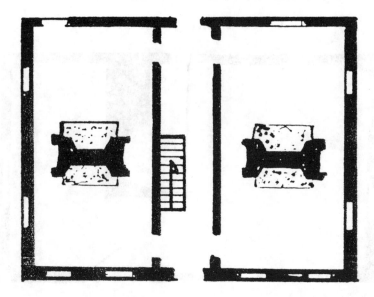

show the evolution and development of housing in America. A more detailed understanding can be found in materials listed in the References section on page 59.

Vernacular Housing

In addition to the basic housing styles that developed between 1620 and 1900, vernacular styles developed in response to geographic, economic, and social conditions of the early settlers. Local building characteristics provide students ample opportunities to study houses unique to their own communities. Virtually every region in the United States has examples of vernacular housing.

Northern New England, for example, has the telescope house and barn, or the connecting barn. This style of building is found nowhere else in the country. The connecting barn allowed residents to walk from the main house through a connecting shed (usually a woodshed) into the barn, sheltered from the cold and the snow that dominated New England winters.

When the early colonists spilled out of their snug cottages built along the eastern seaboard and into the advancing frontier, they built log cabins. "The availability of trees was the principle factor contributing to the widespread distribution of log housing, but the fact that no nails or spikes were needed to build a log cabin, or to erect a log stockade, was an advantage of the utmost importance," writes C. A. Weslager (1969, 6). Log cabins were first built by Swedes and Finns, who settled in southwestern New Jersey and Delaware. Within a few years, William Penn founded Pennsylvania and attracted Quakers, Dunkards, and Mennonites, all of whom built log dwellings as well. From these early origins, the log cabin followed the flow of western migration. When the Scotch-Irish arrived in America, they wasted no time in imitating the log cabins of their Swedish and German neighbors, "exhibiting an adaptability singularly lacking among the earlier Anglo-Americans" (228). Log cabins were inexpensive to build and the materials were in abundance. They still survive today from Pennsylvania to Texas.

History caught up with Texas. Early Texan architecture was heavily influenced by Spanish culture and traditions. By the 1820s, Anglo-Americans began to settle into the area known as Texas today. Three architectural periods dominated the early history of Texas: frontier-settlement architecture, antebellum South, and American Victorian. A natural shift can be seen from the early log cabin and the log house to the more gracious antebellum style. Log cabins were made of round logs and log houses were made of hand-hewn square-cut logs. With the addition of a front portico and clapboards, these modest structures developed an elegant style. Texans made money in cotton, cattle, and lumber after the Civil War. To show off their newfound wealth, they built garish Victorian homes. Turrets, tiled mansard roofs, gingerbread porches, and elaborate materials truly separated this style of architecture from the earlier periods. It was during this period "that architecture was the primary means of expressing wealth, pride, ambition, and self-satisfaction" (Alexander, 8).

Long before the arrival of the Europeans, the Anasazi built great apartment complexes in Mesa Verde, Colorado. Between the sixth and twelfth centuries, the Anasazi constructed a series of villages, individual houses, and cliff dwellings. They moved from a nomadic life of hunting to a sedentary existence of cultivating corn, beans, and squash. These changes were mirrored in the dwellings they constructed. "One cannot view Cliff Palace, Balcony House, Spruce Tree House, or the Sun Temple without sensing the 'ghosts' of past owners. Nowhere in the American Southwest is the 'silent presence' [of the Anasazi] more strongly felt than along the steep walls of the many canyons that slice the high tablelands of the Mesa Verde" (Wenger 1980, 201).

North and west of Mesa Verde lies Paradise Valley, Nevada, in the dry and difficult environment of the Great Basin. Its buildings best exemplify vernacular housing. "The buildings of Paradise Valley arise from the interplay on the landscape of settlement history, ethnicity, customary behavior, oral tradition and ranch life" (Marshall 1995, 9–10). It was settled in the 1870s by Italian Catholic stonemasons, Native Americans, old-stock Americans, German immigrants, Hispanics from California, Basques from Spain, and Chinese from San Fransico. This cultural mosaic determined the architectural style of the buildings in the valley. Adobe-brick one-story ranch houses and granite-block barns were the dominant styles.

When the Old World skills of the Italians, the Basques, and the Hispanics were applied in Nevada's New World environment, they established an architecture that synthesized the cultural and physical landscape.

Activity: Build a House

This activity introduces students to building methods and other considerations housewrights employed when they planned houses for their local settlements. Students will recognize the influence of geography as well as the cultural origin of the builder on the structure. As students plan, design, and build a scale model of a period house, they will appreciate the skill, the time, and the work required to build even a modest structure.

Phase I: Create a House Plan and Description

Architects draw and plan houses all the time. Your students need to do the same. In order to accomplish this, arrange visits to a historical museum, a historic house, or preferably, a historic building in your community. If this cannot be done, create a Tour of Homes slide or Power-Point presentation. It is important for students to see old houses. Require each of them to sketch or photograph a house that interests him or her and write a description to include the following:

Exterior: The paper should describe the type of roof, the pitch, the chimney placement, the number and the location of windows, the type of exterior, and any features that seem unusual.

Interior: The paper should include the number of fireplaces, the room size, the ceiling height, the wall treatment, the type of floor, and the way glass is used.

Site: The paper should describe how the house is situated in relation to the sun and other houses.

The student's description of the house should include a series of tentative hypotheses that explain the reasons for the construction materials that were used, the location of the windows, the roof pitch, the chimney location, and so on.

Phase II: Develop Hypotheses

Now encourage the students to test their hypotheses by conducting further investigations. At this point, the teacher should present a list of topics for students to research that will enable them to confirm or reject their explanations. A partial list follows:

1. Architectural styles in New England and the middle and Southern colonies
2. A period of style (i.e., the Georgian house in the South)
3. The influence of the Dutch, the Swedish, the German, the Huguenots, and the Anglo-Saxons on building styles

Additional reports may include particular houses, interior design, architects and builders, migration patterns, the influence of the Spanish in the Southwest, the French in Louisiana, the Industrial Revolution, and so on. Through student analysis and reports, class discussion and teaching, students are open to a world of housing that probably never existed to them before. This investigation also provides a foundation for beginning to understand our social and cultural value systems.

Phase III: Construct a House

The most exciting part of this activity is when students build a scale replica of a Colonial house. I used *The Timber Frame Planning Book* by Stewart Elliot (1978) because it provides excellent drawings and plans. My experience building houses with my students taught me a few things I want to share with you. First and foremost, our students are not housewrights; they are more comfortable using computers and playing video games. Unless your school offers a course in industrial arts that teaches tool safety, you will need to spend time teaching basic safety.

Before embarking on this activity, consider the following questions: (1) How much time will this activity take? and (2) When can I teach it? My school sponsored a Wednesday-afternoon activity program. It was created so all the adults who worked at the school would take a group of students with similar interests and conduct an activity for them. For instance, the home economics teacher taught her students how to make Early American quilts, others taught basic photography, and I taught building old houses.

You will need the following tools to complete the model house: backsaw, coping saw, drill, chisels, and block plane. To save time, I asked a parent who was a builder if he would be willing to cut the stock to basic dimensions for the students. I personally don't like the idea of watching students rip lumber on a table saw. He agreed. Once the stock was cut, we were ready to scale and build a house. Here are the steps to follow:

1. Students working in cooperative groups select a house style: Cape Cod, center-chimney Colonial, or saltbox.

2. Students create a scale drawing of the house. A good standard scale is $1'' = 1'$. Most houses were $36' \times 24'$, $40' \times 24'$, or $32' \times 24'$. These are easy measurements to scale.

3. Students determine how many sills, plates, posts, and rafters they will need, based on their drawing.

4. Several different joints are employed when building a house. Students will need to make half-lap, mortise-and-tenon, and dovetail joints in order to construct their house. *The Timber Frame Planning Book* provides drawings of these joints.

5. Students begin and end their house the same way it was built by the original settlers—from the bottom up. They cut the bottom sills and put them together with half-lap joints. Since manual dexterity is not fully developed for most students, you can expect some frustration. The first few joints will not necessarily reflect perfection.

6. Your students should build their houses in the style of a good old-fashioned house-raising. Build a frame at a time. When several are

complete, raise them onto the sills and connect them with the appropriate joinery. Soon students will be placing rafters to create the roof.

7. When several houses are ready, you can begin to plan a Colonial community.

References

Burchard, J., and A. Brown-Rush. 1961. *The Architecture of America: A Social and Cultural History.* Boston: Little Brown.

Denison, A., & W. K. Huntington. 1987. *Victorian Architecture of Port Townsend Washington.* Seattle, WA: Hancock House.

Elliot, S. 1978. *The Timber Frame Planning Book.* Chicago: Contemporary.

Elliot, S., and E. Wallas. 1977. *The Timber Framing Book.* Kittery Point, ME: Housesmiths.

Horwitz, T. 1998. *Confederates in the Attic.* New York: Pantheon.

Marshall, H. W. 1995. *Paradise Valley, Nevada: The People and Buildings of an American Place.* Tucson: University of Arizona Press.

Pratt, R. 1949. *A Treasury of Early American Homes.* New York: McGraw-Hill.

Smith, K. G. E. 1976. *A Pictorial History of Architecture in America.* Vols. 1 and 2. New York: American Heritage.

Wenger, G. R. 1980. *The Story of Mesa Verde National Park.* Mesa Verde, CO: Mesa Verde Museum Association.

Weslager, C. A. 1969. *The Log Cabin in America: From Pioneer Days to Present.* New Brunswick, NJ: Rutgers University Press.

Whitehead, R. F., and F. Brown. 1977. "Chocteau and the Early American Society." In *Survey of Early American Design,* ed. by F. B. Chocteau. N. Stratford, NH: Arno.

Williams, H. L., and O. Williams. 1957. *A Guide to Old American Houses: 1700–1900.* New York: A. S. Barnes.

———. 1957b. *Old American Houses: 1700–1850.* New York: Bonanza.

Zeller, T. 1984. "Using the Visual Arts to Interpret the Community." In *Community Study: Applicants and Opportunities.* National Council for the Social Studies Bulletin No. 73. Washington, D.C.: National Council for the Social Studies.

Chapter Five

Using Primary Sources

One of the most exciting ways to engage students in the study of local history is to use primary sources. Memoirs, letters, documents, tax records, news articles, advertisements, art, and photographs are materials that can help students connect to the past. In writing about primary sources, Thomas E. Felt (1976) cites three qualities that show accuracy in the representation of a historical event:

1. *Closeness.* The source closest to the event in time and space, if not an actual observer or participant.

2. *Competence.* The source most capable of understanding and describing a situation.

3. *Impartiality.* The source with the least to gain from distortion of the record. A source may lack impartiality either by reason of a willingness to allow omissions and additions deliberately, or by reason of emotional involvement in the event. (7)[1]

Ideally, a person who witnesses an event and either tells about it in an oral interview or writes about it would seem to be a reliable source. Unfortunately, it is not that simple. For example, if a person survived the great hurricane of 1938 but did not write about it until 1948, the ten-year lapse would cloud initial impressions. On the other hand, a newspaper account of the 1938 hurricane written during the storm would be a more reliable source.

A letter from a doughboy in 1917 might provide an accurate description of life in a trench, but it would not be helpful in assessing overall military strategy. Competence refers to the ability of an individual to understand a situation.

A lot of primary sources are impartial. Tax records, for example, merely record who paid taxes and how much they paid. Most birth and death records simply report information. Statistics compiled by local and state agencies are good examples of reliable primary sources. Eyewitness accounts that become part of a profile can be problematic. Photography, on the other hand, presents a more accurate account of a historical situation.

The rest of this chapter focuses on using photographs as primary sources, illustrating how they can be used to teach students about labor conditions in local communities. Several examples of children working will demonstrate how photography can be used to teach critical-thinking skills. Each activity will meet Felt's criteria of closeness, competence, and impartiality.

Coal Towns

Coal mining is well documented as one of the most dangerous occupations in industrial society. Between 1908 and 1935, 50,000 U.S. miners died extracting coal. Mine explosions were commonplace and attracted much attention. Miners lived in dread of "coal damp," or methane gas, which could be ignited by a spark from a shovel and erupt in fast-moving flames. In a West Virginia mine in 1907, 366 miners lost their lives in a single explosion. Miners also feared a creeping death from carbon monoxide fumes and took canaries down in the mines with them as an early warning system.

The vast majority of miner deaths were actually the result of slate falls. These occurred when a miner cut a wedge into a coal wall and drilled above it to place a dynamite charge; the weight of the rock above the wedge could cause it to cave in prematurely. A curious phenomenon called "bumps" emerged in the mines of Harlan County, Kentucky, during the 1930s. Bumps were a "sudden violent explosion of coal from one or more pillars accompanied by a large report and earth tremors."[2] Apparently, the drive to extract coal faster caused companies to leave too few pillars of rock standing to support the mine ceiling safely.

In spite of the danger, underage boys became miners along with their fathers. Coal operators found hiring boys profitable because they could be paid a fraction of adult wages. Most boys working in the mines were between ten and fourteen years old. Although progressive reformers succeeded in getting some states to pass laws limiting child labor to ten hours a day, enforcement of even this minimal effort to protect children was near to impossible. Typically, a boy could work longer if his parents signed a miner's release swearing he was at least fourteen, and employers could be held responsible only for "knowingly" breaking the law.[3]

Most youths were breaker boys who spent their days sorting coal from slate as cars from the mine were unloaded down a chute in an

unending stream of rock. One of the safer jobs in the mine, it never-
theless exposed these boys to asthma from constant dust, curvature of
the spine from bending over all day, and occasional death or maiming
by the machinery. In the film *Harlan County, USA,* which documents a
strike by Harlan coal miners in the 1970s, an elderly man recalls his
days in a breaker room:

> Well, we breaker boys would have our feet in the chute and we'd be
> picking the slate out when the breaker boss would sneak up behind
> us, and if he saw a piece of slate coming through, he'd pick up the slate
> and hit you in the back with it, and hit you hard. He'd say, "Pick up
> that slate."[4]

Breaker boys were truants from school, noted a reporter for a labor
newspaper: "They play no games; when their day's work is done they
are too tired for that. They know nothing but the difference between
slate and coal."[5]

Breaker boys were not the only ones who suffered the effects of
exploitation; the social structure of their communities suffered as
well. "By the third decade of the Twentieth Century," writes historian
R. D. Eller, "the Jeffersonian dream in Appalachia had become a night-
mare of exploitation, corruption and social tragedy. While the southern
mountains remained a predominately rural area, changes in land ownership, economy, and the political system had left people dependent,
impoverished, and powerless within a new alien social order."[6]

Harlan County, Kentucky, was an especially hard case even before
the labor troubles of the Depression era. In the 1920s, its homicide rate
surpassed that of any other county in the United States, and was "seven
times as high as Al Capone's Chicago."[7] The reasons for this are complex but may center on the recent development of the coal industry in
this pocket of eastern Kentucky. In the first two decades of the century,
the county's population had increased more than sixfold, from 10,000
to 64,000, with miners and their families constituting 61 percent of the
population. Signs that the family structure was breaking down included
an unusually high divorce rate (one in four marriages) and a growth in
child desertion.

Decades of abuses by coal operators led to strikes, violence, and social disintegration. Government studies during this period documented
the collapse of local communities. In *Coal Towns,* historian Crandall A.
Shifflett points to two significant conclusions of the various governmen-
tal investigations: (1) the "standardized living and working conditions"
of company towns "quickly and ruthlessly" destroyed old cultures and
(2) company towns "created a system of closed, artificial communities"
that limited the growth of social freedom and self-determination.[8]

Although conditions for the miners of Appalachia improved somewhat as New Deal reforms took effect (the United Mine Workers were

able to organize 92 percent of the mines in Harlan after passage of the National Industrial Recovery Act in 1933), the Harlan County miners and their families were undoubtedly the victims of a great social tragedy extending over many decades—and, some would argue, into the present day.[9] Their agrarian way of life became an anachronism, and they were forced to adjust overnight to an industrial system that ignored their dignity, stripped them of all vestiges of their former independence, and failed to compensate them by recognizing any rights inherent in their new roles as industrial workers.

Activity: Teaching with Pictures

The graphics in this section represent two periods in the transformation of parts of Appalachia from a rural farming society to an industrial coal-producing region.

"Miners' Children and Houses Near Hazelton, PA" (Figure 5–4) is a stereopticon view made by the Keystone View Company in 1903. Two other photographs, "Tipple Boy" (Figure 5–1) and "Group of Boy Coal Miners" (Figure 5–3), were taken by Lewis W. Hine in 1908 to document the working conditions of child miners for the National Child Labor Committee. "Miners' Families Awaiting News" (Figure 5–2) dates from 1914 and is probably a news photo.

The drawing by Seymour Fogel (Figure 5–5) was made in Harlan County, Kentucky, in 1934, during the decade of labor strife between miners and coal operators. Fogel was an artist with left-wing sympathies who worked with muralist Diego de Rivera and later painted murals for the WPA Federal Art Project.

Provide students with copies of this chapter and ask them to study the pictures and read the accompanying captions. Then ask students to choose one of the following activities.

Activity 1: Using Pictures As Primary Sources When using graphics as a primary source in history, it is important to consider not only the subject itself but the artist's intention and use of technique in presenting the subject. Choose one photo or drawing from this chapter and describe it in terms of its

- Historical content (including any background information about the picture or the photographer/artist)
- Ideological content (Does the picture appear realistic? Does it appear to reflect a particular intention of the photographer/artist? Or both?)

Figure 5–1

A tipple boy poses at the Turkey Knob Mine in MacDonald,
West Virginia, in 1908. A tipple was the apparatus used to empty coal
from loaded cars at the top of the mine. Lewis W. Hine took this
picture to document child workers for the National Child Labor
Committee. Photo courtesy of International Museum of Photography
at George Eastman House.

Photo by Lewis Hine

Figure 5–2

Family members await news of the fate of miners entombed by an explosion at the New River Collieries, Eccles, West Virginia, in 1914. Photo courtesy of the Library of Congress.

Figure 5-3

Breaker boys at a coal mine in Pennsylvania or West Virginia circa 1908–1910. Photograph by Lewis W. Hine for the National Child Labor Committee. Photo courtesy of the Library of Congress.

Figure 5–4
Miners' children stand in front of stripped earth and company
houses in a town near Hazelton, Pennsylvania, circa 1903. This is
a stereopticon view made by the Keystone View Company.
Photo courtesy of the Library of Congress.

- Technical content (any aspects of making this picture that appear
  to have been chosen to convey a particular meaning)
- Emotional impact as you perceive it

Activity 2: Using Pictures to Promote Inquiry Adopt the role of an
investigative reporter who is working with the photographer/artist
who created one of the pictures in this chapter. Use the picture to create a set of questions you would like to ask the person(s) portrayed in
the picture. (For example, what would you ask to learn more about

Figure 5–5
In 1934, Seymour Fogel sketched this view of labor strife
in Harlan County, Kentucky.

child miners, life in a company town, or the labor strife in Harlan County during the 1930s?) You can extend this activity to create a full interview between the reporter and the person(s) in the picture.

Child Labor in Company Towns

Children not only worked in coal mines but in the glassmaking industry, the canning industry, and textile mills. "Between 1890 and 1910 census reports, the number of working children between the ages of 10 and 15 rose from 1.5 million to 2 million."[10] In 1904, the National Child Labor Committee was founded in New York City to investigate child labor in the United States. Though diligent in its efforts, the NCLC report was not well received. Opponents included Southern mill owners, supporters of states rights, laissez-faire economists, and President Woodrow Wilson. By 1912, the Children's Bureau was established to document working conditions of children, and in 1916 the Keating-Owen Bill was passed, establishing standards for working children.

Minimum standards included:

1. Minimum age of fourteen for workers in manufacturing
2. Minimum age of sixteen for workers in coal mining
3. Maximum workday of eight hours
4. Prohibition of nighttime work for children under sixteen
5. Documentary proof of age

Lewis Wickes Hine (1874–1940) worked on the staff of the NCLC as a documentary photographer. A sociologist and humanist, he is best known for his insightful portraits of immigrants at Ellis Island and his views of housing and labor conditions in the United States. As a member of the NCLC, he traveled across much of the southern and eastern states documenting the working conditions of factories, fields, mines, mills, and canneries that made use of child labor. His photography eventually led to the establishment of child labor laws and safety laws for all workers.

Activity: Using Photographs to Describe Working Conditions

Provide your students with a set of photographs portraying children at work in your community. These can be obtained from your local historical society or you can use the Lewis Wickes Hines website. As

Figure 5–6

Photo by Lewis Hine, National Archives

members of an investigation team, students list the standards they will set for child labor in their photographs. The following questions should be addressed.

1. Is the work area safe for workers?

2. Is the lighting adequate?

3. Would you recommend that workers wear protective clothing? If so, what?

4. Should there be a minimum age limit for this task? If so, recommend one.

5. Would you recommend that the children in the photograph be allowed to continue to work at this job? Why or why not?

(Adapted from *The Progressive Years 1898–1917*)

Child Labor Today

Many of your students work. The fast-food chains survive and prosper on part-time help. How many businesses provide employment opportunities in your community and how many students are engaged in

Figure 5–7

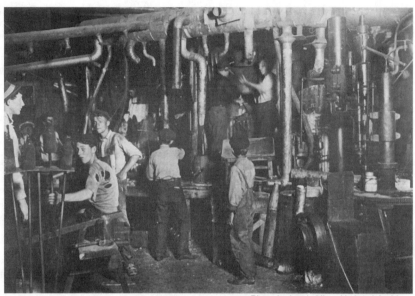

Photo by Lewis Hine, National Archives

Figure 5–8

Photo by Lewis Hine, National Archives

that workforce? "Fifty-nine years after Congress outlawed child labor in its most onerous forms, underage children still toil in fields and factories scattered across America,"[11] report David Foster and Farrell Kramer in *Secret Child Labor in America*. Their report, conducted in the year 2000, lists the following abuses:

- In the past five months, The Associated Press found 165 children working illegally in 16 states, from the chili fields of New Mexico to the sweatshops of New York City.

- They are children such as Angel Oliveras, 4, who stumbled between chili pepper plants as tall as his chin in New Mexico's fall harvest. Children such as Vielesee Cassell, 13, who spent the summer folding and bagging dresses in a Texas sweatshop. Children such as Bruce Lawrence, at 8 already a three-year veteran of Florida's bean fields.

- Although the number of children traced to any one company was small, there are uncounted thousands of boys and girls like Angel, Vielesee and Bruce. No one knows just how many because no one, the federal government included, has tried to count them all.

- To make an estimate, the AP had Rutgers University labor economist Douglas L. Kruse analyze monthly census surveys and other workplace and population data collected by the federal government.

- His study estimates that 290,200 children were employed unlawfully last year. Some were older teens working a few too many hours in after-school jobs. But also among them were 59,600 children under age 14 and 13,100 who worked in garment sweatshops, defined as factories with repeated labor violations.

- Close to 4 percent of all 12- to 17-year-olds working in any given week were employed illegally.

- Employers saved $155 million in wages last year by hiring underage children instead of legal workers.

- Kruse's study could not account for all children who work illegally because available data are limited. For example, census-takers, like labor enforcement agents, have trouble finding the very kids who are among the most easily exploited: children of migrant workers, illegal immigrants and the very young.

- Look to a bustling street in New York City's borough of Queens, where Koon-yu Chow, 15, was found stitching dresses at a garment factory sewing machine last summer. Dresses were being made for Betsy's Things, a label sold at Sears, until state labor investigators inspected the place and Betsy's Things took its business elsewhere.

- Walk into Grayson Sewing in Sherman, Texas. There, Vielesee was one of seven children federal investigators found folding and bagging dresses up to 12 hours a day. All seven were under 14; the youngest was 9. J.C. Penny acknowledged making two purchases of garments from Grayson, a company investigators called a sweatshop.

Activity: Child Labor Survey

Since many high school students work part time, create a survey that would reveal not only the nature of work students engage in but their attitudes toward it as well.

Conduct a Child Labor Survey

Survey:

Name _____

Employer _____

Hours per week _____

Hourly rate _____

Explain the nature of work (i.e., washing dishes, stocking shelves, etc.).

_____

Describe what safety precautions your job requires (i.e., safety glasses).

_____

Describe your work satisfaction. _____

How do you use your income? _____

Does your job affect your school work? What GPA do you currently have?

© 2001 by Robert L. Stevens from *Homespun*. Portsmouth, NH: Heinemann

Notes

1. T. E. Felt, *Researching, Writing, and Publishing Local History,* (Nashville: American Association for State and Local History, 1976), 7.

2. C. A. Shifflett, *Coal Towns* (Knoxville, TN: University of Tennessee Press, 1991), 104.

3. M. B. Schnapper, *American Labor: A Pictorial Social History* (Washington, D.C.: Public Affairs Press, 1972), 277.

4. Interview in *Harlan County, USA,* a 1976 documentary film produced and directed by Barbara Kopple and released by Cabin Creek Films. It won the 1976 Academy Award for Best Documentary.

5. Quoted in Schnapper, 274.

6. Eller, *Miners, Millhands, and Mountaineers: Industrialization of the Appalachian South, 1880–1930.* (Knoxville: University of Tennessee Press, 1982), 5–6.

7. Hevener, *Which Side Are You On? The Harlan County Coal Miners, 1931–39.* (Urbana: University of Illinois Press, 1978), 23.

8. Shifflett.

9. In 1965, the poverty rate in Appalachia was one in three; by 1990, the rate had been cut in half. The largest pockets of remaining poverty are in West Virginia (most of the state), eastern Kentucky, southeastern Ohio, and northeastern Mississippi ("Developing Appalachia," the *Washington Post* [July 5, 1999]: A19). Caudill contends that even today "in social and economic terms there are two Appalachias. One is made up of the people who live there, a few of whom are wealthy and the rest poor by national standards. The other, the corporate Appalachia of the combine, is very, very rich . . . Eastern Kentucky is a colony owned and managed by absentee landlords" H. M. Caudill, *Theirs Be the Power: The Moguls of Eastern Kentucky.* (Urbana: University of Illinois Press, 1983), 151.

10. *The Progressive Years 1898–1917* (Boca Raton, FL: SIRS) 28.

11. D. Foster and F. Kramer. *Secret Child Labor in America.* <http://members.aol.com/_ht_a/munmei/labor.html>.

Teaching Resources

Fiction

Dos Passos, J. 1996. *U.S.A.* New York: Library of America.

Giardina, D. 1992. *The Unquiet Earth.* New York: W. W. Norton.

———. 1999. *Storming Heaven.* New York: Fawcett.

Llewellyn, R. 1997. *How Green Was My Valley.* New York: Scribner.

Stegner, W. 1990. *Joe Hill: A Biographical Novel.* New York: Penguin.

Film

Harlan County, USA
Matewan
The Molly McGuires
How Green Was My Valley

Websites

Appalachian Regional Commission (ARC): <www.arc.gov>

Eckley Miners Village (My Trip to): <sheffner.home.pipeline.com/ecjley.html>

United Mine Workers of America (UMWA): <www.umwa.org>

The Miriam & Ira Wallach Division of Art, Prints and Photography: Photography Collection: <wysiwyg://22/http://www.nypl.org/research...e/art/photo/hinex/workport/biography.html>

Secret Child Abuse in America: <http://members.aol.com/_ht_a/munmei/labor.html>

Chapter Six

Oral History

What better way to learn history than from a story, an anecdote, or an observation by someone who participated in or witnessed the event? Since the 1970s, when accounts of Appalachian life written by high school students through oral interviews were published in the Foxfire Series, interest in using oral history has captured the imagination of many teachers. Social history—history that is not written in textbooks—has appealed to students because they can actually speak with someone who was there. The lives of ordinary people and their everyday experiences, as well as some not so ordinary people and not so everyday experiences, are the focus of oral history. These witnesses to history can provide insights into events such as the Great Depression, WWII, Korea, the Cold War, and the '60s, that tumultuous decade of civil rights, space, assassinations, and Vietnam, in a way textbooks cannot. People have benchmarks or turning points in their lives when an experience is so overwhelming that it forever changes the way they view their own reality. Catastrophes such as a tornado, a hurricane, a serious accident, or in the case of my generation, the assassination of President Kennedy, are such benchmarks. Personal experiences such as hardship, joy, frustration, and patriotism are found in the stories of ordinary folks who witnessed history in the making.

One of the many stories my grandfather, a WWI doughboy, delighted in telling my family was his experience traveling to Washington, D.C., to demonstrate for the Veterans Bonus. After spending a year in France with the Yankee Division, he felt entitled to the promised bonus. After all, he said, "we won the war." In 1924, Congress enacted a law over the veto of President Calvin Coolidge that was a form of veterans insurance based on length of service and overseas service. My grandfather qualified for a plan that allowed him to receive a certificate that would mature in twenty years. According to his account, Congress promised to invest money in the fund each year so the WWI veterans could look forward to an insurance premium due in 1945.

However, the economic collapse of 1929 sent the country into a financial tailspin. By 1932, the financially strapped Congress proposed an early buyout, relieving it from an obligation it could not fulfill. This became known as the Veterans Bonus. Veterans throughout the country, realizing they might lose their promised compensation, began to organize. My grandfather hitched a train to Washington in June 1923 to demonstrate with other WWI veterans. He wore his uniform and camped with other former Yankee Division soldiers in a park near the Capitol. He recalled with pride that this group of demonstrators called themselves the Bonus Expeditionary Force, after the AEF (American Expeditionary Force) that liberated France. Government troops marched in to evacuate the BEF. They burned tents and beat up many of the demonstrators—"our own army," my grandfather said with disgust. He eventually made his way home, and for the next seven years, barely eked out a living until the Great Depression slowly ground to a halt. According to him, "it wasn't until FDR got us out of the Depression" that his faith in government was restored.

Like myself, your students have valuable resources they can tap at home, over the phone, or through e-mail—relatives who were part of history, relatives who perhaps have not told their stories. It wasn't until the year 2000 that Brig. Gen. Paul Tibbets, retired, commander of the Enola Gay, gave an interview describing his experience as the man who dropped the A-bomb on Hiroshima. Stephen Ambrose (1998) found this is not uncommon for many veterans when writing his book *The Victors: Eisenhower and His Boys: The Men of World War II.* Many of our students have grandparents or relatives who served in WWII, Korea, Vietnam, Desert Storm, and the Balkans who could be interviewed to find out what they learned from history.

Oral history is not only about wars and national events. It is about people—men and women of all races and creeds who struggled to meet the day-to-day challenges wrought by difficult times as well as the joys brought on by realized dreams. Students can look forward to a variety of narratives. *Countdown to the Millennium,* an oral history project and radio series based in Ohio, describes four categories student interviewers will often research.

1. **Hardship stories:** These accounts describe experiences with adversity due to poverty, illness, or personal misfortune. Many stories from the Great Depression will fall into this category.
2. **Hazard stories:** These accounts describe how people survived the dangers of a changing economy, world events, or disasters.

3. Golden Age stories: These create a romantic view of the past: things were cleaner, society was better, and our children were better behaved. These memories need to be corroborated with other sources to ensure accuracy. Perceptions change with age.

4. Adventure stories: These tales describe a remarkable experience or the achievement of a major goal.

When students begin to recount their stories like these from their interviews and projects, they will begin to appreciate the efforts of past generations. More important, they will gain a sense of place in that continuity of events we call history.

In addition to relatives serving as resources for oral history projects, stories from members of the community as well as those already transcribed can be incorporated into local history lessons. During the Great Depression, the Federal Writers Project conducted interviews across the country, collecting more than ten thousand stories between 1935 and 1942. About three thousand oral histories are now available through the American Memory Collection *American Life Histories, 1936–1940* (1998). An excerpt from a meatpacking worker will show how valuable this collection can be for developing lessons.

Packinghouse Worker
Marge Paca, 24-years-old
Irish, married to a Pole union member

by Betty Burke

June 15, 1939

Text of Interview:

The meat specialties, that is about the coldest place in the yards. That's where they prepare medical extracts from meats, for hospitals, I guess. Anyway, they have a room there that's 60 degrees below zero. Nobody is supposed to stay there longer than 3 minutes, but some of the men go in there for 15 minutes at a time.

I used to have to pack the brains in cans. They would be frozen stiff and my nails would lift right up off my fingers handling them. It's always wet there and very, very cold. I had to wear two and three pairs of woolen stockings, 2 pairs of underwear, a couple of woolen skirts and all the sweaters I had, and on top of that I had to wear a white uniform. My own. But I couldn't stand it there, it was so cold. It's easy to get pneumonia in a place like that.

In cleaning brains you have to keep your hands in ice cold water and pick out the blood clots. They have the most sickening odor. Cleaning tripe, though, that's the limit. Rotten, yellow stuff, all decayed, it just stank like hell! I did that for a few weeks.

Then I worked in the sausage department. In the domestic sausage. We'd have to do the pork sausages in the cooler. Sometimes we wouldn't be told what kind of sausage we'd have to work on and then when we'd come to work they'd say 'pork to you' and we'd have to throw any dirty old rags we could pick up around our shoulders and go to work in that icebox. If they had any sense or consideration for the girls they could let them know ahead of time so that girls could come prepared with enough clothes.

In summer sausage, they stuff very big sausages there. That's very heavy work. A stick of sausage weighs 200 pounds, five or six sausages on a stick. They have women doing that. It's a strong man's job and no woman should be doing that work. The young girls just can't, so they have the older ladies, and it's a crime to see the way they struggle with it. On that job I lost 27 pounds in three months. That was enough for me. It's a strain on your heart, too. Women got ruptured. They pick the strongest women, big husky ones, you should see the muscles on them, but they can't keep it up. It's horses' labor.

In chipped beef the work is much easier. You can make better money, too, but the rate has to be topped, and it's very, very fast work.

Interview transcriptions like this one create a number of possibilities for teachers. The account itself is sobering. It portrays a slice of life most students are unfamiliar with, about working under intolerable conditions. You have the opportunity to extend this vignette and many more like it into related activities such as higher-level thinking questions, diary entries, or journalistic accounts of work in America.

Before we get ahead of ourselves, let's remember that this was the last step in the oral interview process, a final transcription. How should you begin an oral history activity with your students? I have found the Federal Writers Project model is similar to many strategies.

Gather Background Information

Students who are not prepared for a speaker or an interview cannot possibly benefit from the experience. Developing questions and being able to interpret the response require content knowledge of the topic under investigation. For example, interviewing a coal miner without knowledge of mining operations, hazards, life in mining communities, and labor/operator problems would not yield fruitful results. One of the best ways to address this problem is to incorporate your oral history project into the curriculum unit you are teaching. During the time you plan to teach the Great Depression, for instance, would be an appropriate time to interview seniors who witnessed that period in history. Your students should be familiar with the economic conditions that led to the crash, the government policies of the time, and the plight of many Americans left in the wake of the crash. Once this umbrella of knowledge has been established, students can then inquire into how these events affected the lives of individuals in their communities.

Develop Questions

Have your student imagine it is 1936 and they are interviewers for the Federal Writers Program. What kinds of questions would they ask? Here are some possibilities:

- What did your family eat today? Where did the food come from? In Nebraska, Russian thistle soup was not uncommon; in Georgia the monotony of grits was the staple.

- Who supported your family and how? Since unemployment was high, many Americans worked for a variety of federal programs, notably the Civilian Conservation Corps.

- How did people in your community cooperate with each other? Did they? What ways did they help each other?

- What did people do for entertainment? How often did they participate?

- How did people get from one place to another? What mode of transportation was most often used? Can you tell me a story about something that happened to you when you were traveling from one place to another?

- Did your family members vote? Who did they vote for? Why?

In addition to the general questions created about the Great Depression, your students will need to develop specific questions. The general questions serve as a warmup; they will create a rapport with the speaker and allow him or her to let old memories surface. For example, I was asked to speak at a women's luncheon on the Great Depression. My slide presentation combined art and photography of the period. Immediately after the talk, several women began to recount their experiences. I left an hour and a half later after listening to many poignant stories.

An online search will help most students zero in on their topics so they can ask more specific questions once their subjects begin to open up.

1. Tell students to use specific keywords in their word search. The narrower, the better: *CCC* as opposed to *federal work programs,* or *Farm Security Administration* as opposed to *Depression photographers.*

2. Select three or four sources and then decide if you have enough information to compile a list of good questions.

The Interview

If your students are not able to contact someone in their families to interview, you can invite guest speakers to your class or put students in contact with potential interviewees. There are many organizations that are more than willing to provide speakers to schools. Veterans groups, civil rights activists, Peace Corps volunteers, antiwar demonstrators, and people involved in political campaigns are excellent choices. Senior citizens centers are another valuable resource for oral history projects.

On the day of the interview, your students will need to review their prepared questions and check the tape recorder if one is to be used. If students won't be taping the interviews, it is a good idea for one person to conduct the interview and a second to take field notes for later transcription. The Federal Writers filled out forms as part of their interviews. Their subjects were called informants. They included the following information in their write-ups:

Ancestry

Place and date of birth

Family

Place of residence

Education

Occupation and accomplishments

Special skills and interests

Community and religious activities

Description of informant

Once the interview is completed, several opportunities exist for using the data students have compiled. Teacher Andrea S. Libresco has her students incorporate oral history interviews into a research paper. (See her article "Doing REAL History: Citing Your Mother in Your Research Paper" in Part II.) Several teachers I have worked with have their students conduct interviews with civilians and veterans from the Vietnam era. Students arrive in class dressed according to the people they interviewed and discuss and debate the war. In my own class, I had students create an FDR Fireside Chat. Participants described their plight as a result of the economic collapse. All of these possibilities allow students to transcribe their oral interview notes into a product. Not only does this fulfill higher-level thinking skills suggested by Bloom (1956), but it also conforms to the NCSS Essential Skills for Social Studies: Organizing and Using Information Standard, which says students need to be able to synthesize new information and communicate orally and in writing.

References

Ambrose, S. 1998. *The Victors: Eisenhower and His Boys: The Men of World War II.* New York: Simon & Schuster.

American Memory Collection. 1998. *American Life Histories, 1936–1940.* Historical Collection for the National Digital Library. Washington, D.C.: The Library of Congress.

Wigginton, E., ed. 1991. *Foxfire, 25 Years.* New York: Anchor.

Chapter Seven

How to Get
from Here to There
Maps and Their Uses

A map is worth a thousand words. It explains and shows not only how to get there from here but also what one can expect along the way. *Cartographical Innovations: An International Handbook of Mapping Terms to 1900* (Wallis and Robinson 1987) lists 191 entries consisting of eight specific groups of maps:

1. Types of maps
2. Maps of human occupations and activities
3. Maps of natural phenomena
4. Reference systems and geodetic concepts
5. Symbolism
6. Techniques and media
7. Methods of duplication
8. Atlases

Each group and specific map furnishes the user with great detail, enabling students to better understand information not provided in any other format. In spite of the immense variety of maps, the central concept students will learn is that all maps are symbolic representations of a particular worldview. This view is affected by cultural attitudes and technology. Although similarities exist among maps, cultural differences give each map its uniqueness.

Map activities will help your students learn basic map skills and reinforce the five basic geographic themes.

1. Location: This is probably the most obvious use of maps. Absolute and relative locations can easily be seen by using maps and a globe. Distance between locations helps students develop an awareness of travel time, whether for an early explorer attempting to circumnavigate the globe or for a modern family from Seattle, Washington, traveling to Mesa Verde, Colorado.

2. Place: Topographical maps reveal where we are—on a plain, a hill, or a mountain. Climatic maps contain data concerning temperature and precipitation. Population maps indicate the density of people living in specific areas and at particular times. Using these three types of maps, students can develop hypotheses about specific places. What kind of place is it? Would they like to live there? What can be done to make it a better place to live? Is it possible to make it better? All of these questions ask what the human and physical characteristics of the place are.

3. Region: Maps can help students identify and create regions. They find characteristics common to an area and pinpoint a region. The Corn Belt, the Rust Belt, the Dairy Belt, and the Pacific Rim are a few examples of well-known regions. However, investigative minds can create new regions. Students can identify areas where religion, language, economic activity, climate, river systems, rail lines, and so forth intersect.

4. Human-environmental interaction: What happens when people migrate into a previously unsettled area? If trees are cut and farms developed, how does that affect the environment? Or conversely, what happens when people decide to reforest an area? From the earliest civilizations along major river systems to our present densely populated centers of trade and commerce, humans have had an impact on the environment. At what cost? The fragile balance between human settlement and the health of our natural environment is a major concern as we move into the twenty-first century. Maps provide students with problem-solving activities that will enable them to suggest and predict possible future outcomes. What have we learned from the poor farming practices of the 1930s that created the Dust Bowl? Is deforestation in Brazil going to create similar conditions in Latin America, as might the unprecedented harvesting of old-growth forests in America's Northwest? What are the economic and ethical questions raised by human development? Time lines and maps aid in the comprehension of such complex problems. They can demonstrate the impact

human activity has on the environment and promote a new way of thinking about the future.

5. Movement: Migrations of peoples can be easily understood by students when they are visually represented. Movement allows students to investigate the push-pull factors that are responsible for population displacement. Movement is not only a human condition but also includes physical elements in the environment. The slow but relentless movement of the Sahara Desert in Northern Africa is creating problems such as desertification. Shorelines in coastal zones are also affected by the movement of the oceans. The extent to which these conditions affect human populations is another set of problems that students can analyze.

Activity: Salem Witchcraft Trials

This activity will help students understand the effects of conformity, order, and obedience in a community. In 1692, a devastating explosion of hysteria ripped the very fabric of Salem Village. Adolescent girls accused local citizens of practicing witchcraft. This led to the execution of 19 innocent people and the imprisonment of 150 more. What actually happened and the reason for it have been the subjects of research by numerous historians and writers. I find two resources extremely useful in helping students understand this time period: *The Crucible*, a play by Arthur Miller, and *Salem Possessed: The Social Origins of Witchcraft* (1974), an analysis by Paul Boyer and Stephen Nissenbaum.

In concert with performing *The Crucible* or particular scenes from it, it is helpful to present a series of maps so students can better understand community relationships. The following maps are adaptations from *Salem Possessed*.

A brief history is in order to fully understand the dimensions of the 1692 accusations. In 1672, Salem Village was granted the right to establish a church. For years, it had petitioned the General Court for this status. Like many New England towns, most people wanted to separate from bigger communities and obtain permission to hire their own ministers because of the great distances they had to travel to meeting houses. In Salem, the distance was not only in terms of actual miles but also, and more important, in terms of the value systems. Geographically, Salem Village was inland and agricultural, reflecting conventional values of the times. Ideas and changes in attitude were slow to affect the lives of Salem Villagers. On the other hand, Salem Town had established mercantile ties with London and the Caribbean. Ideas were

Figure 7–1
Salem: Town and Village.

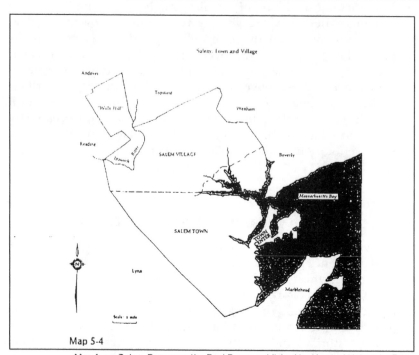

Map from *Salem Possessed* by Paul Boyer, published by Harvard University Press

disseminated quickly. The profits from trade changed the lives of the inhabitants of Salem Town, and the gulf between village and town began
to widen (see Figure 7–1).

Though political boundaries suggest the similarity of interests
(states, nation, etc.), these are never clear-cut. A second look at Salem
Village in 1692 reveals an interesting pattern. Ask students to determine any pattern that might exist (see Figure 7–3). Students will see
that Salem Village is almost divided in half regarding the witchcraft
accusations. It is interesting to note that the accused witches and their
defenders lived closest to Salem Town and the ocean. Do witches and
their defenders prefer larger towns and the ocean? Or are there other
explanations? Other maps will be needed to help students answer the
question.

The tempest that struck in 1692 moved through the community
like a hurricane, expanding and gradually uprooting all aspects of early
Colonial village life. The accusations moved from the center at Salem
Village to include persons as far away as Boston. The initial conflict
stemmed from the debate over hiring Samuel Parris as minister of Salem

Figure 7–2

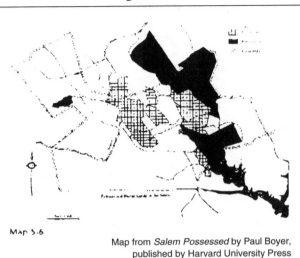

Map 5.6

Map from *Salem Possessed* by Paul Boyer,
published by Harvard University Press

Village in 1689. Internal village bickering and squabbling over the terms of his contract, property, and even the amount of wood he was provided sowed the seeds of destruction.

Two maps illustrate the residential patterns that existed just before and after the witchcraft accusations. Two prominent Salem families, the Porters and the Putnams, were involved in the dispute of Samuel Parris and the witchcraft accusations. (For a complete analysis, see Boyer and Nissenbaum 1974, 110–37). Though they each had almost identical histories and land holdings, these families found themselves in opposite camps (see Figure 7–2).

Ask students to compare Figure 7–3 with Figure 7–2. What are their conclusions? Is there any relationship between Porter property and the witchcraft accusations? Are the defenders of the witches Porters or persons sympathetic to the Porters? What motives might the Putnams have to accuse people of witchcraft? Are these people who are being accused actual witches?

After the trials, imprisonments, and executions, the hysteria finally subsided, bringing in its wake some interesting geographical patterns: "In April 1695 an ecclesiastical council meeting at Salem Village, under the leadership of the Reverend Increase Mather, hints that Parris should resign; eighty-four of Parris's Village opponents petition the council members to take a stronger stand" (Boyer and Nissenbaum 1974, xvii). In May, the council members recommended more forcibly that Parris resign; 105 of Parris' village supporters signed a petition in his behalf. In June, the Salem Village Church endorsed Parris, who served as minister until the following July, when he resigned. It is interesting to note

Figure 7–3
The Geography of Witchcraft: Salem Village.

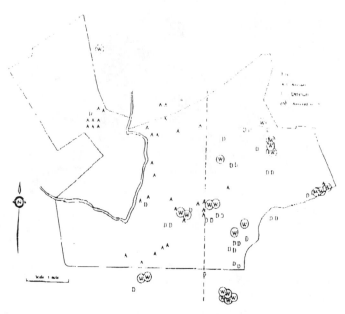

Map 5-5
Map from *Salem Possessed* by Paul Boyer, published by Harvard University Press

where the supporters of each faction resided throughout the pro-Parris and anti-Parris petitions of 1695.

Ask students to count the number of pro-Parris and anti-Parris supporters in the section that is marked off by dashed lines in Figure 7–4. What conclusions do they draw from this analysis?

Figures 7–1 through 7–4 help students understand some of the aspects of a very complex social problem. It is clear that geographical patterns begin to shed light on the witchcraft hysteria. In addition, other questions for further research should be considered. Which individual people were accused? Initially, the accused were women who were considered deviants or outcasts in the community: Tituba, a West Indian slave, Sarah Good, a pauper, and Gamma Osborne, a bedridden old woman. As the accusations increased, a broader range of villagers were included, though one pattern remains clear: people opposed to the Reverend Parris were the subject of accusations.

Maps provide a lot of rich information when students learn how to analyze them. "Geography was and is more than a background or backdrop to historical events and processes. The nature of our understand-

Figure 7–4

The Geography of Factionalism: Residential Pattern of the Signers
of the Pro-Parris and Anti-Parris Petitions of 1695.

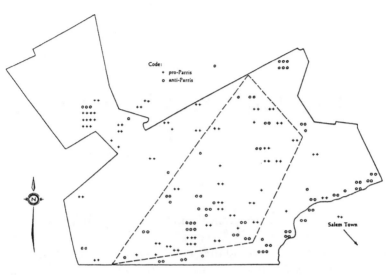

Map 5-7

Map from *Salem Possessed* by Paul Boyer, published by Harvard University Press

ing of space and spatial relationships is of consequence, and historical atlases provide a means for assessing how these have changed over time" (Black 1997, ix). Incorporating map activities in a local history lesson or unit helps students gain a more informed assessment of their community's past.

References

Black, J. 1997. *Maps and History: Constructing Images of the Past.* New Haven and London: Yale University Press.

Boyer, P., and S. Nissenbaum. 1974. *Salem Possessed: The Social Origins of Witchcraft.* Cambridge: Harvard University Press.

Wallis and Robinson. 1987. *Cartographical Innovations: An International Handbook of Mapping Terms to 1900.* England: Map Collector Publications.

Chapter Eight

Write Your Family History

Where did your ancestors come from? Did they arrive on the May-flower or on an overcrowded ocean liner in 1910? Are they Italian, Irish, or Old Yankee? Why did they come to America? Every family has a history and a story. This genealogical activity presents your students with an immediate problem, but because of its generative nature, it can also provide them with a lifetime of research and pleasure. In the process of writing a family history, your students will become interested in aspects of history, economics, geography, and psychology that affected the lives of their ancestors. More important, they will begin to understand their relationship to history.

Incorporating the Geographic Themes

The five geographic themes (*Guidelines for Geographic Education* 1984) can be employed in helping students investigate their own families. Ask your students to locate precisely where particular family members lived and when. Use pushpins on a world map to show where family members live today. Once each student has located the origin of his or her family, ask him or her to describe what kind of place it was. This task involves research. Students should answer the following questions:

1. What was the environment like?
2. What economic conditions led to emigration?

3. Were family members persecuted for social, political, or religious reasons?

Since our students reflect a multicultural society, this activity will provide a base for better understanding of what students have in common and as well as reasons for understanding and accepting differences.

Once your students can describe the places in which their ancestors lived, they are ready to investigate the reasons that made them leave. Push-pull factors drive people across countries and over continents. Student research will reveal reasons their ancestors left their homelands. What risks did family members take in the hope of bettering their condition? Every subculture in America has its unique set of circumstances, and every student is a product of cultural heritage. A well-researched family history today will help students find connections to their past.

New cultures washed upon the American continent in successive waves. As the population pressed westward, spilling into every corner of our country, Native Americans were displaced, rivers polluted, timber cut, and land exhausted. In short, the once pristine character of our country was severely altered. What impact did immigration have on our land as industrial society was created? What problems exist today? How should they be solved? The human-environmental interaction is a powerful theme that can be used in this activity. It provides students and teachers with immeasurable lesson possibilities.

We the People: An Atlas of America's Ethnic Diversity (Allen and Turner 1988) illustrates the fact that America is composed of ethnic regions. Although boundaries are not clear-cut, students will find that specific ethnic populations settled in particular areas of the country. The largest concentration of Native Americans live in the Southwest and in the northern tier states of Oregon, Montana, North and South Dakota, Minnesota, Wisconsin, and New York State. Students with French ancestry will probably live in northern New England or Louisiana, whereas German and Scandinavian descendants most likely live in the upper Midwest.

The West Coast reflects ethnic diversity more than any other region in the country. Spanish influence dominated early in California's history. More recently, Chinese, Japanese, Koreans, and Southeast Asians have immigrated to the West Coast. What factors were responsible for these regional patterns of immigration?

You can seize the opportunity to encourage students to conduct further research or teach lessons that show the relationships between your students' ancestors and larger regional or national events. Swept along in a wave of history, ancestors were subjected to many forces. Several examples will serve to illustrate my point.

1. Do some of your students have Irish names? Quite possibly, their families came to America during the 1840 Potato Famine in Ireland. The economic forces that contributed to a major migration, the impact the Irish have had on America, and the ways in which the Irish were initially received are bits of the cloth of America's fabric.

2. Perhaps some of your students' families are Franco-American and lived and worked in the New England mills after emigrating from Canada. What events caused them to move? How did they maintain their cultural and religious heritage after arriving?

3. Perhaps their families are African American and live in the North. Did their families migrate from the South, or are they descendants of the first black slaves in the North? Did they leave the South after the Civil War, or were they some of the few who escaped slavery through the Underground Railroad?

4. My great-grandmother had a piece of silk from the Orient that she had received from her great-grandfather, who was a ship's captain. Her mother's maiden name was Mary Ann Townsend. In the process of attempting to determine if I am related to the famous War of 1812 privateer Penn Townsend, I learned a lot about local history as well as national events.

Researching a family's history poses many questions for further investigations. Why did the family move? Why doesn't the town they lived in exist anymore? What effect did wars, economic conditions, family struggles, deaths, and so on have on family members? Once the pot begins to boil, it will continue to simmer throughout a lifetime.

The rest of this chapter is divided into the following five topic areas. Mastering these areas will enable a student to conduct a family investigation in the manner of a professional genealogist.

1. Pedigree chart
2. Family history
3. Research
4. Problems
5. Interdisciplinary activities

Pedigree Chart

A pedigree chart is a visual representation of one's family. Similar to a map, it provides structure and direction. Students can easily see the relationship between a great-grandmother on the maternal side and an

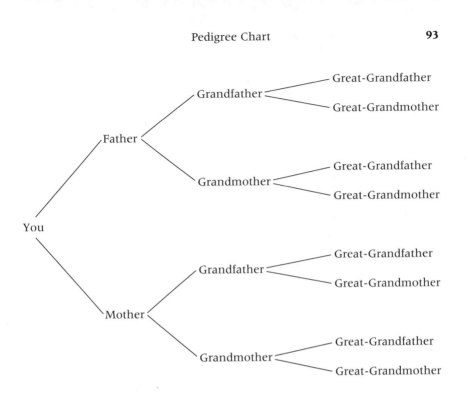

uncle on the paternal side. In this way, students can trace and understand bloodlines. Two types of pedigree charts are the common ancestor chart and the present generation chart.

I feel the common ancestor chart is best for your students to use because it begins with them. The present generation pedigree chart is used as a formal instrument when the activity is complete. The working chart is just that: during the stages of inquiry, students use it for notes, comments, or leads. The present generation pedigree chart is presented first.

Research begins at home. Students fill in the chart, listing when and where family members were born, married, and died. When the chart is as complete as possible, the next phase begins, in which students collect data on family members and the institutions to which they belonged. For this activity, students will want to use a working chart. The chart allows them space to record family members and vital dates. In conjunction with the chart, they should keep an organized notebook or cards to record pertinent information.

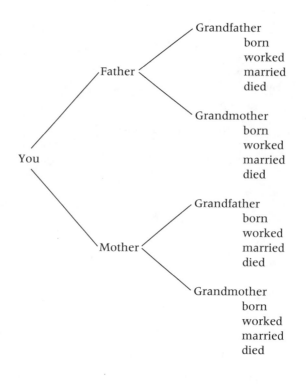

Family History

Family members are often the best source for gathering information for a family history. Usually someone has kept family records, collected newspaper clippings or made scrapbooks, or retained possession of the old family Bible. Have students seek that person out. As the web is spun, it will eventually encompass older, distant relatives. Third cousin Margaret may have photographs of a family reunion taken in 1925 or a hastily penned note concerning her Aunt Nett's bout with yellow fever. Family tradition is a good source for the beginning student re-searcher. Information gathered from the present generation is easy to obtain and confirm. However, as one steps back into the lives of earlier ancestors, the anecdotes are less reliable and more difficult to corrobo-rate. Once a relative has told a version of an event or recounted a story told to him or her, it is time to check the information. No matter how believable some stories seem, they main contain inaccuracies. Gilbert Doane (1960), in his book *Searching for Your Ancestors*, relates a story written by an aged grandmother on the history of her family.

Here is all Grandma can think of about the forefathers. Lord John
Whiting, Great-Grandfather, was born in 1735, near London. He came
to America on the May Flower in 1776 soon after the Revolutionary
War, bringing his two daughters Lady Jane and Mabel (Not sure of the
name). She, Mabel, went back to England with her father.

Lord Whiting bought some land in Connecticut and gave it to Lady
Jane for a wedding present when she married Grandfather James
Dupey. He was a French nobleman in 1796 or 1798. James Dupey was
Captain of the May Flower. Ten sons were born to them. (30–31)

Students should ask the following questions to verify information:
Are the dates correct? Do other sources state similar claims? Some sto-
ries will provide amusement as well as information, as does this one:
"John the sone of John Warnor and of Mahittabel his wife was borne
December ye: 18th:1716; Daniel ye sone of John Warnor and of Mahit-
tabel his wife was born May ye:6th:1717" (Doane 1960, 8).

After conversations with relatives have been exhausted, students
can start searching through family records. Family histories, bulletins
or organizations, and family Bibles contain information that is usually
accurate. The family Bible recorded the important events in one's life and
often had notes scribbled in the margins. Based on Jones, Eakle, and
Christensen (1972), the survey in Figure 8–1 suggests an infinite number of family sources that can be used to obtain information on relatives.

Research

By now your students have amassed a lot of information using the
pedigree chart and family records. Of course, there are gaps. Bloodlines might appear to terminate because no one could recall a great-
grandfather's mother's maiden name. Determine what they should do
next. Do students want to follow their mother's family or perhaps
spend time researching one generation in the 1840s? Help them define
their research objective.

Family research is complex and exceedingly time-consuming. Encourage each of your students to select one *manageable* aspect of his or
her family that is intriguing and bear in mind the following guidelines:

1. Select a family problem.
2. List sources that are accessible.
3. Determine a realistic time for completion.

An actual investigation will serve as an example. In my family, so
the story goes, at the age of eleven, Great-Great-Uncle Page Sumner sat
in an apple tree and watched the Confederate army advance through
the Manoghesey Valley and engage in battle with Union troops. Did

Figure 8–1
Survey Outline.

Survey Outline

Pedigree Ancestors   *Birth Date and Place*

_____

_____

_____

HOME JURISDICTION: (Immediate, Family, Friends, Close Relatives, Associates)

Those I Can Personally Visit   *Those I Must Correspond With*

_____

_____

_____

HOME SOURCES:

This checklist is a guide to the records you should find in the homes of your relatives. Check (√)
each record you use. Write additional sources you may discover in the empty blanks.

Personal Records	*Legal Papers*	*Certificates*
Journal	Will	Birth
Diary	Deeds	Marriage
Biography	Land grants	Death
Patriarchal blessing	Water rights	Divorce
Letters	Mortgages	Adoption
Seal	Leases	Graduation
Photographs	Bonds	Christening
Autograph albums	Loans	Blessing
Personal knowledge	Contracts	Baptism
Baby book	Summons	Confirmation
Wedding book	Subpoenas	Ordination
Scrapbooks	Tax notices	Transfer
Funeral book	Guardian papers	Ministerial
Guest register	Abstracts of title	Mission release
Travel account		Membership
Treasures of truth		Apprenticeship
Book plates		Achievement
		Award

Military Records	*Family Records*	*Financial Records*
Service	Bible	Accounts
Pension	Books of remembrance	Bills
Disability	Family group sheets	Receipts
Discharge	Pedigrees	Check stubs
National Guard	Genealogies	Estate records
Selective service	Temple record books	
Bounty award	Family bulletins	
Service medals	Family histories	

SURVEY OUTLINE (*continued*)

Military Records
_____ Ribbons
_____ Sword
_____ Firearms
_____ Uniforms
_____ Citations
_____ Separation papers
_____

Citizenship Papers
_____ Naturalization
_____ Denization
_____ Alien registration
_____ Deportment
_____ Passport
_____ Visa
_____ Vaccination
_____

School Records
_____ Diplomas
_____ Report cards
_____ Honor roll
_____ Awards
_____ Transcripts
_____ Yearbooks
_____ Publications
_____

Employment Records
_____ Apprenticeship
_____ Awards
_____ Graduation
_____ Citations
_____ Severance papers
_____ Social Security
_____ Retirement papers
_____ Pension
_____ Union
_____ Income tax
_____

Family Records
_____ Printed histories
_____ MS histories
_____ Local histories
_____ Family traditions
_____ "Birth briefs"
_____

Announcements
_____ Wedding
_____ Birth
_____ Death
_____ Funeral
_____ Graduation
_____ Divorce
_____ Anniversary
_____ Memorial cards
_____ New job
_____ Travel
_____ New home
_____ Birthday
_____ Professional
_____ Engagement
_____

Newspaper Clippings
_____ Anouncements
_____ Obituaries
_____ Special events
_____ Vital statistics
_____ Hometown papers
_____ Professional
_____ Trade
_____

Membership Records
_____ Cards
_____ Publications
_____ Programs
_____ Uniforms
_____ Awards
_____ Certificates
_____

Health Records
_____ X-rays
_____ Insurance papers
_____ Hospital records
_____ Medical records
_____ Immunizations
_____

Licenses
_____ Business
_____ Occupation
_____ Professional
_____ Hunting
_____ Firearms
_____ Driver's
_____ Motor vehicle
_____

Household Items
_____ Silverware
_____ Needlework
_____ Sampler
_____ Tapestries
_____ Dishes
_____ Friendship quilt
_____ Coat of arms
_____ Insignias
_____ Souvenirs
_____ Clothing
_____ Tools
_____ Memorial rings
_____ Engraved jewelry
_____

Books
_____ Atlases
_____ Yearbooks
_____ Textbooks
_____ Prizes
_____ Treasured volumes
_____ Vocational
_____ Foreign language
_____

Uncle Page Sumner actually witness the battle? To determine if he did, I followed this inquiry plan.

What Sources Are Accessible?

1. Interview the family members who told the story. Do dates and times check with history?

2. To determine when and where the person lived, check family histories, letters, birth and death certificates, church records, and census data. For example, was Uncle Page eleven years old during the Civil War and did he live in the Manoghesey Valley?

3. Look at newspaper accounts and other records from the time. For example, I studied Civil War documents.

4. Write a narrative describing the family member and the event he or she observed, assuming other sources confirm the story.

What Is the Time Frame?

1. Plan time for local research.

2. Plan time to send and receive letters from distant family members.

3. Is the family traveling to visit relatives or the city or town in which events unfolded?

Problems

You will find genealogical research is fraught with problems. Students should not believe everything they read or hear until it has been corroborated and should be particularly skeptical of anecdotes that have filtered down through oral family history. Most of us would rather believe that our ancestor was a famous patriot than believe he was a common crook. Many families are blessed with both. Family skeletons need to be exhumed from closets to keep company with their more honored relatives if accuracy and understanding are to be achieved.

Family tradition is the first problem. Although there is an element of truth in many stories that are handed down, the actual circumstances, when held to close scrutiny, are often quite different from the tale told. In *Pitfalls in Genealogical Research,* Milton Rubicam (1987) illustrates the problem:

> Many English and American families named Hall have traditionally claimed descent from William Shakespeare through his elder daughter Susanna, wife of Dr. John Hall. The fact remains, however, that the Bard of Stratford-on-Avon does not have a single descendant living today. The last member of his direct line was his granddaughter,

> Elizabeth Hall, wife of Sir John Barnard (Bernard) who was buried on
> 17 February 1669/70. (16).

Your students must be wary when using family tradition as a single source.

Another problem that is vexing for student researchers is the confusion that surrounds people with the same name who live in the same place and are approximately the same age. Rubicam cites an interesting example:

> In his article "Too Many Jonathan Gilletts in Windsor Connecticut,"
> *TAG*, 56:72–79 (April, 1980), he listed seventeen men by the name of
> Jonathan Gillett who lived in Windsor from before 1677–1777. These
> include four pairs of brothers who never met each other, the elder of
> each pair having died before the birth of the younger. (34)

In a less complicated example, my own research has located several Townsends who are listed as ship's captains and mariners; who had wives named Mary Anna, Mary Ann, or Marianna; and who lived within three blocks of one another. Time and patience are required to unravel these initial confusions.

In addition to confusion over names and persons, there can sometimes be confusion over words and their meanings. Rubicam has devoted an entire chapter to this issue (37–42). I have taken a few examples from that chapter so you can appreciate the problem: *Mr.* and *Mrs.* were originally reserved for persons of social position. *Master* and *Mister* were the correct attributions and were strictly applied to the landed gentry, members of the clergy, and public officials. *Mrs.* (mistress) was applied to both married and unmarried women. In the eighteenth century, *spinster* was used to designate both wife and widow. Today it has two meanings: a woman who spins thread and an unmarried woman.

Word changes are very elusive. A list of sixty-seven names of occupations is provided in *The Source: A Guidebook to American Genealogy* (Eakle and Cerny 1986, 342). Among them are *ale-draper* (innkeeper), *backster/baxter* (female baker), *Barker* (tanner of shoes), *flescher* (butcher), *Hind* (farm laborer; household or domestic servant), and *wright* (a constructor, such as a shipwright). Changes in language such as the ones listed do arise unexpectedly, but for the neophyte researcher, they can create interest and require further study.

Interdisciplinary Activities

The family is a subject that can be explored in literature and in writing. "Family literature, then, is a piece of writing—prose, poetry, or drama—that emphasizes the family and sees the individual as part of a larger family unit whether over one or several generations" (Gouldrup 1987, 1). Getting to understand families better can be accomplished in several ways. The first is through students' work. A journal or a diary, its pages brown and brittle like autumn's leaves, set the scene for a short story. Imaginative writers create conflict and resolution, and a story is born. Ink-stained, splotchy old letters, Rorschach-like, evoke images that lift the words from the page into poetry, giving students opportunities to let their imaginations wander through the past.

In the second way, students read good literature, poetry, and drama after having struggled with their own pieces. Gouldrup provides an excellent resource list for this purpose in his book *Writing the Family Narrative*. A poem by Edith Mendez titled "Tenement Mother" is an example of the power that is achieved through poetry.

Tenement Mother [1]

Hands chafed by ribbed washboard
she labored late over iron tub
until back and legs gave.
Nights she walked rough wooden floors
tending her brood. Sweet tea
for small complaints, cool hands
for fevered head.
Her heart wore down bearing children
two years apart; one held in arms,
a second tugging at her skirt,
the third kicking in her womb.
Cautioned she would not survive
another birth, her husband said
nature will not be denied.
In her fortieth year she bore
her eighth. Heart broken, she died.

A third way to engage students' interest is to use letters or documents (primary sources; see Chapter 5) found in family archives to generate lessons from the past. When I taught eighth-grade U.S. history in Rye, one of my students brought in a letter that Secretary of State Seward had written during the night of President Lincoln's assassination. Since we had just completed a unit on the Civil War and were familiar with the assassination, students' attention was riveted as I read the letter to them.

Using family letters not only helps students better understand their own family history but is also extremely valuable as a resource for teachers. A distant relative on my wife's side of the family, T. K. West, left for Idaho in the 1870s seeking his fortune. After several unsuccessful years of mining in Idaho, he traveled south to Paradise Valley, Nevada, to work in the silver mines. Three letters and a newspaper article contain all the elements necessary to create a lesson on the Old West.

Please send answer by
Wells, Fargo & Co s Express.

Spring City, Nev.
April 23rd, 1879

Dear Sister and Brother-in-Law:

Your most welcome letter came to hand some time ago and I should have answered it err this but I have bin attending court in Winnemucca for two weeks and have not had a chance to write.

Well, Nannie, I guess I deserved the scolding which you gave me for not writing. The fact is that for the last four years since I left Idaho everything has been so dark for me that I have not had the heart to write to any of my old friends. Amidst all my troubles I have however steadily clung to the idea that the future had something in store for me besides sorrow and disappointment. At the present time everything bids fair for a brilliant future in Nevada. The discovery of the mines here in Spring City is already having a beneficial affect stimulating and creating renewed energy in every department of industry. Capital, substantial capital, both from California and the East, is finding its way in here and being invested every day in rich mines already discovered. One year ago there was not a house in this camp, now there is a town and a population of about 5,000. I am content to stay here though at times the spirit yearns to visit old scenes, friends and associates in Callaway where I passed so many years. I subscribed for the Fulton Telegraph about a year ago and received it regular for a while but long before the time had run out it quit coming. It used to inform me of renewed prosperity of Fulton and occasionally the sad intelligence of the departure of some of those who once were bosom friends for the land of the unknown.

Nannie, I am glad you and Milt have settled down among the friends in Callaway and I am glad you are so well pleased with your home. It must be heart rendering for Nannie West just to think of her mother, father, and sister have all died since she left home. I met with Will last summer in Boys City. He told me that Nannie looked as young as when she left home. They have . . . darling child [or children?], two of the smartest boys out. They have four children one of them I have never saw. They get away with you and Milt raising children. Will told me that . . . took his father's death very hard when I saw . . . some in Battle Mountain. He said he had rather see Nannie than any one on the earth.

Nannie, it is most time for me to get supper. I am working night shifts now and have to go on at six o'clock, come off at three and sleep until ten o'clock. I had my photograph taken while in Winnemucca and I shall send you one and I hope you and Milt will send me yours and also my niece's picture. Nannie, write often to me and if I should neglect to answer immediately you just write again. You have more time to write . . . and I don't want you getting mad about it. I'll give you a good talking to when I get back there.

Remember me kindly to one and all, the kin folks and Mother in particular. Don't fail to write soon to your far off Brother K. West.

Take good care of my dog. He must be getting old and feeable now.

P.S. If the school marm falls in love with my picture just let her send me hers and if she is good looking I'll send her money to come on.

Paradise Valley
May 5

Dear Mother,

By this letter you will see the condition which I am now in. On last evening I attended a little entertainment in this place I met probably with a fatal accident. I will do the best I can to explain to you that I was not at least a blame so you will not entertain any feeling against me if this be my last. I was sitting quietly in my seat when a man came and sat in my lap. I requested him to <u>leave</u> when he turned and struck me over the head with a revolver two or three times. I then left the hall to go out to wash the blood from my face when he followed and shot me in the groin and it is supposed by doctors it entered the bladder. There are two doctors attending me at the present. They say there may be faint chance of my recovery. Dear Mother, I can safely say that I have not an enemy in this place and do not think on the coast. Even the very man that shot me was a good friend an hour before. Mother, I am willing to die if my time has come. I have done nothing wrong, why should I fear death? Dear Mother, if we should meet no more on earth, I hope we will meet in heaven where the bonds of friendship knows no separation and where the word farewell is never spoken. You will kindly remember me to sisters, brother and family.

From your Devoted son
T. K. West

Paradise Valley
May 21st, 1879

Mrs. Mattie V. West,

In answer to your letter of information with regard to your Brother. I can only say you have already heard the worst long ere this. Your Brother died three weeks ago yesterday at half past five in the evening and was buried the following day Wednesday.

You can rest assured that every thing was done for him that mortal's could do during his short but terrible distress. I am a stranger here, came here but a few days before the deed was done, but I know that your brother had a host of friends. He was very nicely interned in the cemetery about one half mile from the town. The cemetery is enclosed with a neat fence and properly cared for. While I am a stranger here, I can say that relatives never did more than did the friends of your Brother to soothe and comfort him. It was the only theme of conversation and all were eager to do but aid was impossible. I have a family living in Van Buren Co., Iowa and as soon as the deed was done, I wrote to my wife about it with orders to have it published in the papers there in hopes you might hear in that way as I learned you lived in Missouri. With this I close but should you desire to ask any questions for further information you can address one and I will answer with pleasure.

J. H. Hellwig

FULTON TELEGRAPH
May 23, 1879

A COLD-BLOODED MURDER.

Thomas Karey West, of Callaway County, the Victim.

His Death-Bed Statement.

The Heart-Felt Sorrow of Sympathizing Friends Expressed in a Letter of Condolence to His Beloved Mother.

We copy the following account of the deeply afflicting murder of our young friend, T. Karey West, from the (Paradise Valley, Nevada) *Reporter.* He was a native of his county and son of Mrs. Rowena West, residing six miles west of Fulton, on the Columbia road, near White Cloud church. We sympathize with the family and relatives on their sad and un-looked-for bereavement:

At about 11 o'clock on last Sunday night, May 4th, during the performance of Mlle. Henri's Burlesque Troupe in Kemler's Hall, occurred one of the most brutal and cowardly murders ever committed in any community. The facts are as follows:

The name of the murderer is Charles Hymer, a young man about twenty years of age, who, during his stay in these parts, has been trying to get up a reputation as a desperate man, never missing an opportunity to pick a quarrel with, and abuse some drunken or defenseless man. The name of the murdered man is Thomas K. West, a young man about twenty-four years of age, a peaceable and law-abiding citizen, and one who gained the respect and confidence of all with whom he became acquainted. During his long stay in this town he was never known to have a quarrel with any one, and a wrong or mean act cannot be brought up against him.

Toward the close of the performance the manager announced that the entertainment would conclude with the Parisian Can-can, for the purpose of permitting any person in the audience who did not desire to see it, an opportunity to withdraw. A number of ladies were present, occupying front seats, and immediately upon the announcement of the concluding piece, arose and left the hall.

The vacant seats were immediately filled by young men from the rear seats. When the ladies had retired, Hymer went to the front, and using very filthy language, called, "Bring on your Can-can!" He was immediately called to order by the manager, Mr. Loraine, and requested to keep quiet or leave the hall. He then threw all the blame on Pat Flynn, an old man who had not made a single remark of any kind. He next sat down in West's lap and was asked by him (West): "Charley, can't you find a seat? I can't hold you; sit somewhere else." Hymer got up and remarked that he would "sit where he d—d pleased," and seated himself on the arm of the chair occupied by West, for a few moments, and then dropped into West's lap again. Placing his hands under Hymer, West gently raised him up and said: "Charley, find a seat; I can't see the stage through you." Hymer, placing his hand in his hip pocket, drew a pistol, and with the words, "son of a b—," struck West several times over the head. With the last blow, the pistol fell from his hand, caused by striking over too far. A crowd, among whom was the deputy sheriff, rushed forward and separated them. A short time afterward, West told Hymer he would "like to see him a moment," and started for the door. Hymer still holding the pistol in his hand behind his back, went out with him, followed by George White. At the door, West turned around and said: "Charley, why did you abuse me so? You certainly had no reason for it." The answer was, "You son of a b—, I'll show you," accompanied with a blow and a pistol shot by Hymer. George White seized Hymer, threw him down and took the pistol from him, thus preventing a second shot. The shot fired took effect in West's right groin and ranged to the left. Dr. Powell was sent for, and expressed but little hope. Dr. Bogman was also sent for, and arrived Monday, but no human power could save the unfortunate man's life. Kind friends, of whom there were many, made his last moments as easy as possible.

There were about 150 persons in the hall at the time of the trouble, who became very much excited, and a large portion of the most influential and substantial men of the valley were for hanging Hymer. The rope was got and horses hitched to a wagon, preparatory to lynching, when other counsel prevailed. It was truly a miracle that he escaped lynching, and had it been known that West would die, nothing but Supreme interference could have prevented his neck being stretched.

About 4 o'clock Monday morning Deputy Sheriff Morse and Messrs. Adams and Riddle, by private conveyance took Hymer to Winnemucca and lodged him in the county jail. It is said that he showed no remorse for what he had done until after the heavy iron doors of the jail were closed upon him, when he trembled and shuddered frightfully. When asked what was the matter, he replied that he was "very cold all over," notwithstanding the day was very warm.

His preliminary examination took place at Winnemucca last Thursday before Justice Osborn, and he was held over without bonds to await the action of the Grand Jury.

At the post mortem examination, which was conducted by Dr. Bogman and Dr. Powell, it was found that the ball, after entering the body at the right groin, passed into the abdomen, just missing the bladder in its course toward the left side of the body, where it struck the internal surface of the left hip bone and glanced upward and backward, passing immediately behind the intestines. Owing to the extensive adhesions and engorged condition of the intestines, the ball was not followed further than eight or ten inches in its course, and consequently was not found.

On Tuesday evening, the 6th inst., the sufferings of poor murdered West were perminated by the merciful interposition of death, and on the day following, his remains were consigned to the earth, followed by the lasting regrets of the many to whom his brave and kindly heart had long endeared him. His funeral, which was very numerously attended, took place from Gillilan's Hotel, and long before the hour appointed, the streets and vicinity of the hotel were thronged with people from the Spring City and the outlying portions of the Valley— came to witness the last sad rites, and to pay the last tribute of esteem to their murdered friend. The business houses were all closed, and an air of the deepest sadness and depression pervaded the hears of all, being so manifest everywhere, that Wednesday will be long remembered in Paradise Valley as a day of gloom and general mourning.

The following named ladies contributed and assisted at the dressing and laying out of the murdered man: Mrs. L. Abel, a handsome lace trimmed pillow for coffin; Mrs. G. A. Middleton, cross of flowers; Mrs. Charles Kemler, wreath of flowers.

At 3 o'clock the funeral cortege formed the hotel, and upon reaching the quiet little graveyard, again formed in mournful silence around the newly made grave. Milo Craigin, A. S. Burbank, Jr., J. Miller, Theo Rappell, H. B. Davis, and A. B. Chittick acted as pall bearers, and the beautiful services of the dead were conducted by J. B. Case, assisted by the Paradise school choir, and were impressive in the extreme. At the solemn words, "Ashes to ashes, and dust to dust," the tears stole unbidden to every eye, and as the body was given to the earth, the weeping became audible, and hushed was the sound of the mattox and spade, unbroken the stillness, except by the sobbing, and the earth was placed softly on the breast of poor West. Lingering long around the grave, the mourners sadly and silently departed, leaving the spot to the kindly memories that will ever hover near it.

Thomas K. West was a native of Missouri, and a young man in the flush of health and vigor. He was hard-working and industrious, honorable in all his dealings, a faithful friend and genial companion; brave as a lion in the face of danger, but tender and sympathetic as a woman in the presence of pain and sorrow; ever ready to aid and assist, even to impoverishing himself. His affectionate nature and manly traits of character had so endeared him to the residents of the valley that one might search in vain for a man occupying the same humble position that he did, and yet so well and favorably known, esteemed and respected.

Beautiful and pure as the flowers o'er his untimely grave, in memory's garner treasured, long shall live the kindly thoughts of brave, honest, faithful T. K. West.

Letters of sympathy were forwarded to his mother.

PARADISE VALLEY,
MAY 6, 1879

Interdisciplinary activities that encourage your students to use their families as the basis for a piece of creative writing, reading about other families, and creating lessons from family letters all serve to help your students place themselves in the context of family history. It is here that they see their connection to the past. Many of our students' families offer rich opportunities to learn from the past, stories that should be shared with their fellow classmates.

Connecting Family History to National History

T. K. West's demise falls prey to our perceptions of the Wild West, a West replete with Billy the Kid, the Daltons, and Wyatt Earp. Writers and artists, not to mention Hollywood, have helped shape our collective vision of the West. At the time of T. K. West's murder, Frederic Remington, an Eastern illustrator, was sending images of the frontier to his editors in the East. Americans at the time hungered for accounts of frontier life. The palette of cowboys, soldiers, trappers, and Indians that Remington portrayed in such publications as *Harper's Weekly, The Century Magazine,* and *Youth's Companion* made him one of America's most popular illustrators. Remington's drawings were full of adventure. The account of T. K. West's death in the Fulton Telegraph merely reinforced the public's attitude toward the frontier. What accounted for Remington's romantic perception of the West and the public response to it? Did Remington's illustrations and West's death serve to fill a psychic need—Remington's own and that of others—as Americans far removed from the West came to see what they were about to lose, or had already lost, in the passing of the frontier?

Urban Americans were not interested in the social reality the West represented, and Remington was not dealing with social and economic forces as they existed in reality. Rather, he presented a mythical conception of the frontier, wherein all his subjects became characters in a cosmic drama. Although set in the West, Remington's paintings omit any strong sense of geographical place. Because his characters represent values, the setting is not important. The idea of the last stand—Custer and his men fighting to the end, cowboys shooting it out with Indians—represented to Remington the struggle for white man's values against all odds.

And just what was at stake here? As Hughes (1997) points out: "Turn of the century America was filled with anxiety about immigration: many of Anglo-Saxon stock felt imperiled by the rising tide of racial 'impurity'." He points to Remington's own xenophobia as exhibited in a letter the artist wrote: "Jews, Indians, Chinamen, Italians, Huns . . . rubbish of the earth . . . I've got some Winchesters and when the massacring begins I can get my share of them, and what's more, I will." Remington's West may be seen as a metaphor for mainstream culture standing its ground against the profound social and economic changes being wrought by industrialization and immigration.

Activity: Thinking About the Frontier

The death of T. K. West coincided with the closing of the frontier, as officially proclaimed by the U.S. Census Bureau in 1890 and expounded upon in Frederick Jackson Turner's thesis "The Significance of the Frontier in American History" in 1893 (see Appendix A). In addition, frontier images produced by Frederic Remington were well received by the American public, images based not on reality but on Remington's romantic notions of the West.

Objectives

- To analyze Turner's view of the importance of the frontier in American history by reading excerpts from his thesis (see Appendix A) and answering a series of questions.
- To analyze the frontier art of Frederic Remington by viewing selected pictures and answering a series of questions.
- To place Turner's thesis, Remington's art, and West's death within the broader historical content of the period.
- To describe the difference between myth and reality as it relates to the American frontier and also to explain our strong attachment to a romantic interpretation of the West.

Procedures

1. Students should read excerpts from Turner's thesis and answer the following questions.
   a. How did the U.S. Bureau of the Census define the frontier? Why did it declare the frontier closed in 1890?
   b. What assumptions did Turner make about who owned the West? Document your answer with statements from his thesis.
   c. According to Turner, the wilderness transformed the colonist who entered it. How did he explain this? What assumptions about the American Indian were contained in his explanation?

   d. What view did Turner hold of the Indian trader? What effects on Indian culture did he attribute to this trade?

   e. How did Turner describe the role of the U.S. Army on the frontier? What is the effect of saying the Army had fought a series of "Indian wars"? What if Turner had said that American Indians fought a series of "U.S. Army wars"?

   f. Turner's thesis, both explicitly and implicitly, propounds a theory of social evolution. How is this view presented here? How do you think it might relate to the social Darwinism of his time?

   g. Compare Turner's portrayals of the American and the "Indian." What traits appear distinct to each? What traits appear interchangeable? Do you think Turner saw them as such?

   h. Turner viewed the westward movement as a "procession of civilization." This being so, how does one square his statement that, with the advance of the Indian trader, "the disintegrating forces of civilization entered the wilderness"?

   i. According to Turner, what was the most important effect of the frontier on American history?

   j. Do you agree with Turner that the end of the frontier "closed the first period of American history"? Or are the issues raised by the Turner thesis still alive today?

2. Students should read "Frederic Remington's Image of the Frontier" in *Social Education* (January 2001) and answer the following questions. It would enrich this activity for students to see pictures by Remington and to read the article after viewing the pictures. A good and easily available book on the subject is Matthew Baigell's *The Western Art of Frederic Remington* (1976).

   A Dash for the Timber (1889). Oil on canvas.
   a. What is the geographical location of this painting?
   b. Where is the action in this painting concentrated?
   c. What human qualities does the artist give the cowboys?
   d. How does the artist depict the Indians? (Students may note that they are equipped with rifles.)
   e. Is the painting a romantic or realistic portrayal of the Western conflict over land?

   Fight for the Waterhole (1903). Oil on canvas.
   a. What is the geographical location of this painting?
   b. What perspective on the fight does it present?
   c. What human qualities does the artist give the cowboys?
   d. How does the artist depict the Indians?
   e. Is the painting a romantic or realistic portrayal of the Western conflict over land?

Figure 8–2
A Dash for the Timber.

Figure 8–3
Fight for the Waterhole.

Figure 8–4
The Cheyenne.

The Cheyenne (1901). Bronze statue.

   a. What tribal member does this statue depict? (A warrior.)
   b. What features help define this Cheyenne? (Student responses
   have included "flowing hair," "long spear," "strong leg muscles,"
   and "speed of the galloping horse.")
   c. What human qualities does the artist give the Cheyenne?
   d. What overall impression do you think this statue conveys?
   e. Is the statue a romantic or realistic portrayal of the American
   Indian?

3. Students should compare and contrast the concepts of the frontier
offered by Turner and Remington. What do they have in common?
Do they differ significantly in any way?

4. Students should evaluate the art of Frederic Remington using the
following questions.
   a. What is the relationship between the closing of the frontier and
   the art of Remington?
   b. How do you think Remington's portrayal of the frontier
   reflected and/or affected American attitudes and values at the
   time?
   c. Do you think Remington's image of the frontier still influences
   Americans today? Why or why not?

References

Baigell, M. 1976. *The Western Art of Frederic Remington.* New York: Ballantine.

Ellwood, P. 1974. *The Image of the Indian and Black Man in American Art, 1590–1900.* New York: George Braziller.

Hassick, P. H. 1973. *Frederic Remington.* New York: Harry N. Abrams.

———. 1994. "Frederic Remington's Studio: A Reflection." *Antiques Magazine* November: 666–673.

Hughes, R. 1997. *American Visions: The Epic History of Art in America.* New York: Alfred A. Knopf.

Kendricks, G. 1974. *Albert Bierstadt: Painter of the American West.* New York: Harry N. Abrams.

McCrachen, H. 1959. *George Catlin and the Old Frontier.* New York: Bonanza.

Powe, F. 1998. "Perspectives on the American Landscape: The Conflict Between Native and European American Ideas of Landownership." *Social Education* 62 (3): 126–33.

Truettner, W. H., ed. 1991. *The West as America: Reinterpreting Images of the Frontier, 1820–1900.* Washington, D.C.: Smithsonian Institution.

Note

1. Reprinted from Lawrence P. Gouldrup's *Writing the Family Narrative.* (Salt Lake City, UT: Ancestry, 1987), 69, published by Ancestry Incorporated.

References

Allen, J., and E. J. Turner. 1988. *We the People: An Atlas of America's Ethnic Diversity.* New York: Macmillan.

Clatterbuck, D., and J. Clatterbuck. 1879. Letters Regarding T. K. West. 23 April; 5 May; and 21 May.

"A Cold-Blooded Murder." 1879. *The Fulton Telegraph* 23 May.

Doane, G. 1960. *Searching for Your Ancestors.* Minneapolis: University of Minnesota Press.

Eakle, A., and J. Cerny eds. 1986. *The Source: A Guidebook to American Genealogy.* Salt Lake City, UT: Ancestry.

Gouldrup, L. P. 1987. *Writing the Family Narrative.* Salt Lake City, UT: Ancestry.

Guidelines for Geographic Education 1984. Association of American Geographers and National Council for Geographic Education.

Jones, V. L., A. H. Eakle and M. H. Christensen. 1972. *Family History for Fun and Profit.* Provo, UT: Community.

Rubicam, M. 1987. *Pitfalls in Genealogical Research.* Salt Lake City, UT: Ancestry.

Chapter Nine

Create a Community Image

When you think of your community, what image comes to mind? Do you think of tall buildings stretching like church spires toward the sky? Waves of rustling corn leaves undulating in the gentle wind on a hot summer day? River barges pushing cargo past steel piers and ferrying products to the heartland? Tawny adobe buildings casting long shadows in the last rays of the setting sun? A lichen-covered granite wall framing a town green?

Some images are not so romantic. They are filled with violence and decay: garbage-strewn dark alleys, unlit places, and a brown haze of pollution gently settling over the skyline like a blanket suffocating those who sleep below.

Cities and towns create their own images and have images foisted upon them. From community pride to sports teams to riots, images are in a constant state of flux. The chamber of commerce seeks to create positive images to attract business as well as instill a sense of pride. "Everything is better in Metter," reads the slogan one cannot miss as he or she drives through Metter, Georgia. Newspaper reporters, on the other hand, will create images based upon a single event, sometimes fairly and sometimes unfairly. Pagano and Bowman cite several examples of how cities are viewed in their study *Cityscapes and Capital* (1995). As they point out, "Cities' images are not the same all the time and are not the same to all people" (45). Consider the following images. Are they accurate?

"It's the city of Giants in the Earth, Prince and Garrison Keillor against the city of Scarlett and Black political power and CNN," wrote a *New York Times* reporter during the Minnesota Twins and Atlanta Braves 1991 World Series.

Miami and Los Angeles, cities "built on the power of dreamscape, collective fantasy, and facade" earlier in the twentieth century, have evolved into different images in recent times. Miami is "now the happening capital of the Caribbean, soaked in drug money and a setting for stylish cop shows." L.A. is "mellow, laid back, casual, ever richer, far out, unhurried."

Today, the O.J. Simpson trial and the Rodney King beating remind us of L.A. Elian Gonzalez reminds us of Miami. How much have these events shaped our view of these two cities?

Carl Sandburg's Chicago, "hog butcher of the world," was replaced when Michael Jordan started scoring points for the Chicago Bulls. After Jordan's retirement from the NBA, are we still "bullish" on Chicago, or will it revert to the "Windy City"? Cities are not static; they experience economic decline and revitalization. Shifts in political power and new technologies influence the vitality of cities. Until recently, Boston was imprisoned by its Colonial legacy—historic buildings and old infrastructure. Today, as it responds to the challenges of the twenty-first century, it is becoming the "New Boston." Images can change, too.

Activity: Create a Poster

One activity you can present to students is a chamber of commerce poster contest. Students will need to create a poster about their community that will interest potential businesses to relocate there, encourage parents to live there, or generate civic pride. The poster should include a community slogan. The value of this activity is that students need to think about their community in a reflective way. Also, since it is difficult for most middle and secondary students to incorporate all the information they have learned from a community study and synthesize it into a single sentence or slogan, this is an excellent critical-thinking activity.

Daniel J. Walkowitz (1990) describes New York City as "a tale of two cities." For example, Hollywood films such as *Miracle on 34th Street* and *Breakfast at Tiffany's* conform to our expectations that a city is a magical place in which dreams of opportunity, opulence, and success come true (189). Conversely, *On the Waterfront, West Side Story,* and *Fort Apache: The Bronx* illustrate the dark side of the city, with its crime, gang violence, danger, and corruption.

Atlanta is a city that belies its Georgian neighbors. From its founding in 1842, it continually grew and today is a major American city. Its residents renamed the city from Terminus and earlier Marthasville to

Atlanta (feminine of *Atlantic*) to avoid being considered provincial. My students at Georgia Southern University continually remind me that Georgia is two states: Atlanta, and the rest of Georgia. Bradley R. Rice's aptly titled essay "If Dixie Were Atlanta" (1983) describes Atlanta in the context of the South and the conflict between regionalism and national economic values.

What slogan would your students create for their town or city? Refer to the "Create a Community Image" chart below for some ideas. When students are designing their posters, it is important for them to consider all aspects of their community, from its history, to the positive and negative elements of community life today, to their vision for the future. A mind map is a good exercise to help students think about their community. Two possibilities exist: (1) a chronological time line representing the ebb and flow of the community and (2) a web where specific information is connected to a major theme.

1750	1800	1850	1900	1950	2000

Create a Community Image

Atlanta	"If Dixie Were Atlanta"
Baltimore	"Southern Culture and a Northern Economy"
Dallas/Ft. Worth	"Marketing the Metroplex"
Houston	"The Golden Buckle of the Sun Belt"
Indianapolis	"Silver Buckle on the Rust Belt"
Kansas City	"A City in the Middle"
Miami	"The Ethnic Cauldron"
New Orleans	"Sunbelt in the Swamp"
New York	"A Tale of Two Cities"

Adapted from Bernard (1990) and Bernard & Rice (1983).

Activity: Public Art

Another project that will help students appreciate their community is creating a mural similar to the Public Art that was so prominent during the Great Depression. They should begin by researching the American art of that era and the purposes of that art.

The stock market crash in 1929 brought about the collapse of the American economy. Thousands upon thousands of Americans were left without jobs or homes and trudged endless miles of highway looking for something, anything, better than what they had. Massive dust storms devastated the farmers who could no longer grow enough to keep their own families alive, much less sell crops at market. People were rapidly approaching a state of hopelessness. Something had to be done, and immediately, to rectify the situation.

Out of this chaos and confusion, the Works Progress Administration was created by executive order under the direction of Henry Hopkins with an appropriation of $1.39 billion. One of its stated goals was to improve morale. The WPA created jobs in virtually every sector. Architects were put to work creating new buildings, bridge builders improved the national infrastructure, the Civilian Conservation Corps "took young unmarried men from the relief rolls and put them to work in the woods" (McElvaine 1993, 154), writers were set to work writing guidebooks to the then forty-eight states, and artists were certainly not neglected either. The federal government created the Public Works of Art Project in 1933, a short-lived agency (it lasted only seven months) that was later replaced with the WPA's Federal Art Project. "The Federal Art Project was established in the mid-1930s to create the most notable experiment of the work relief program (McElvaine 1993, 268)." It was driven by economic need, resurgent democratic values, Rooseveltian paternalism, and the quest for a distinctly American culture.

The focus of the PWAP and FAP was not strictly directed toward what would later become the quintessential expression of Depression-era art, namely mural painting; rather, it embraced a broader artistic spectrum. The FAP "gave work to painters, sculptors, graphic artists and art instructors. Its 5,000 artists created some 108,000 easel paintings, 17,700 sculptures, 11,200 print designs, and 2,500 murals" (Bustard 1999, 9). The area of mural art was largely, although certainly not exclusively, administered by the Section of Fine Art (the Section) of the Treasury Department, whose purpose was not only to put the proverbial "starving artists" back to work but to use them as vehicles for the creation of a new American spirit, a new vision of the future, that would transcend the broken-down shacks and dying cattle and uprooted citizenry that characterized the times. As McElvaine aptly states, "They saw Federal One [the FAP] as a grant opportunity to fuse 'high culture' with American Democracy" (1993, 269). The Section and its operations deputy, Edward Rowan, strove for art of a classical, timeless quality that would not so much reflect the dismal reality of the times but create an American artistic renaissance in the truest sense of the word. American Idealism was the product of this renaissance. American Idealism (Fogel and Stevens 1998) was a synthesis of two competing genres during the 1930s: Regionalism (American Scene) and Social Realism.

Regionalism

These painters depicted a romantic or pastoral view of America. They primarily painted in the Midwest and their works represented rural values and themes—a Jeffersonian ideal, replete with scrubbed main streets, aspiring white-steepled churches, bountiful crops, and determined characters—in essence, the last vestiges of a well-ordered agrarian society. Robert Hughes (1997) writes in *American Visions*, "There is a certain irony in the fact that Regionalism, which was promoted as the very essence of American democracy, was the kissing cousin of both official art of the 1930s Russia and that of Germany. If both Stalinist and National Socialist Realism meant images of rural production, green acres, new tractors, straw haired children, and sinewy farmers breaking the sod of the homeland, so did Popularist/Capitalist Realism set forth by Benton and other Regionalists" (455).

The painters and their works clearly reflected the values they embraced, such Regionalism painters included Thomas Harte Benton (*Cradling Wheat* and *The Hail Storm*); John Stuart Curry (*Baptism in Kansas* and *The Gospel Train*); and Grant Wood (*American Gothic, Young Corn,* and *Stone City, Iowa*). Pioneer morality, frugality, individualism, self relience, and religion, basic core American values, embraced Regionalism. After all, they were painting "salt of the earth," Americans from the heartland.

Social Realism

Social Realism, on the other hand, depicted the underside of American life. The Depression created circumstances that forced artists to respond to the tension between American democratic ideals and the social and economic dislocation so evident. As David Peeler observed, "The Depression dashed any such hopes, providing their own hardships and the artists were not immured from worldly problems, and demonstrating with its horrible vistas the irreverence of idyllic paintings. Describing themselves as roused from esthetics reveries, these artists abandoned any pursuit of detached grandeur and committed themselves to Social Realism, a school of art devoted to criticizing the actual world" (1987).

The dark and critical themes painted by the Social Realists reflected their perspective as well. They included Philip Evergood (*American*

Figure 9–1
Lynching by Seymour Fogel.

Tragedy); Jacob Lawrence (*One of the Largest Race Riots in East St. Louis*);
and Seymour Fogel (*Lynching*).

Murals of the Depression

Under the auspice of the Federal Art Project (1935–39), which became
the Art Program of the Works Project Administration of the Federal
Works Agency (1939–42) and ended as the graphic Section of the
War Services Division, both Regionalists and Social Realists survived
economically, but perhaps as important, they created a vision of national art. Holger Cahill, project director of the FAP, and his associates
were firm believers in the ideal of cultural democracy; they expressed
their goal as "art for the millions." Franklin Roosevelt agreed with the
objectives, if not always with the content of the art aimed at the millions. The president guessed—optimistically—that only 10 percent of
the American people had ever seen a "fine picture." For a brief time,
the FAP changed that.

Rooted in the notion that American history provided examples of
challenges overcome and dreams fulfilled, the FAP encouraged artists
who proposed murals to be hung upon school walls, post offices, and

federal buildings to create a sense of optimism and hope. The rules were simple and clear:

1. The subject had to reflect either a historic event or a commercial enterprise that the local community would immediately recognize.

2. The mural could not offend any individual or group in the community. Thomas Harte Benton's *Social History of Missouri*, Edward Laining's *Building of the Union and Pacific Railroad* and Seymour Fogel's *The Relationship of the WPA to Rehabilitation* are examples of murals that won competitions and were placed in WPA buildings during the 1930s.

Some panels were rejected, however. Fletcher Martin's *Mine Rescue*, though bold in conception, masculine in strength, and well balanced in composition, did not survive community scrutiny. The last thing residents in a mining community wanted to be reminded of was the possibility of a mine disaster.

Negro River Music by Gustaf Dalstrom was rejected for other reasons. A composition of several African Americans singing and dancing on a river dock while waiting for a paddle wheeler to arrive too easily fit into the stereotype of lazy blacks.

Figure 9–2

The Relationship of the WPA to Rehabilitation by Seymour Fogel.

Figure 9–3
Mine Rescue by Fletcher Martin.

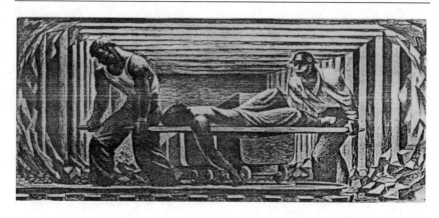

Introduce Public Art to Your Students

One morning in early spring, I left the university in my old black truck and headed north on Georgia's Route 25 to Burke County Middle School in Waynesboro, Georgia. Wayne Hickman, a demonstration teacher, had invited me to do a presentation on Public Art of the Great Depression for his eighth-grade Georgia history students. I had forty slides ordered in the carousel and activity packets for the class but had not yet thought of a good way to really get the students excited about art in the 1930s. To compound this problem, the students lived in a small rural community and did not have the benefit of a visual arts program in their school. I thought of FDR's comment that few Americans had ever seen a "fine" picture.

As I was rehearsing in my mind how I would structure the class, I passed a green-and-white sign welcoming me to Burke County. On either side of the two-lane road were fields under cultivation; some would soon see green shoots of corn and others cotton. Sparsely populated, it was a pastoral setting to be sure—a setting worthy of a Regional painting.

Just over the next rise, my problem was solved. Off to the edge of the highway, twelve black men in white coveralls were picking up trash in front of a large white school bus. Behind them stood a white man in a blue security guard uniform. My second impression of Burke County was the image of a group of black parolees under the watchful eye of a white guard.

I soon turned into the middle school's visitor parking lot, checked in at the main office, and was escorted to Mr. Hickman's classroom. The students were prepared for my visit and were eager for me to view their Depression posters describing the New Deal, the WPA, the CCC, the NRA, and so on. Mr. Hickman wanted them to understand the myriad federal programs initiated during the Great Depression. My intent was to get the students to think about creating a mural similar to the Public Art of the '30s for their community. I wanted his students to think about something they knew, something very familiar to them. I asked them to close their eyes and pretend they worked for an advertising agency. Their assignment was to create an image of their community. It could be a slogan, a picture, or even a song title. After a few minutes, ideas flowed. All of them had contributions.

One young girl suggested a blanket of cotton fields touching the sky; another saw a barn standing tall on the ridgeline; and still another, a bird dog pointing at his quarry (Burke County is the bird dog capital of the world). Their contributions reflected their pride in school and community. This was my starting point. I then asked them what values they thought were imbued in their images. This was a difficult question for them. "Wait just a minute," I said. "We'll come back to this question." The lights were turned off and I projected the first slide on the screen, *American Gothic* by Grant Wood. "Let's talk about this painting," I said. "What do you see?" At first the students were puzzled. Soon, however, a few tentative responses came forth.

"The window in the house looks like a church," quipped a young man.

"Why is that?" I asked.

"The window is pointed like a church."

"Okay, what about the woman? What kind of person is she, do you suppose?"

"Man, she is dull," replied one of the girls. "No fun at a party."

We all spent a few minutes discussing how she was dressed. They agreed she was probably a puritan.

"Not exactly," I said.

"But she is dressed in a somber, frugal manner."

"The gothic window and the three tines on the pitchfork remind us of the religious background of the couple and the dress tells us something about the value of puritan morality," I replied. "Grant Wood wants us to view this couple as hardworking, religious people, the salt of the earth, true Americans."

As I continued to help them analyze the painting, the students seemed to comprehend how an artist injects values into his work.

"Does this painting reflect democratic values?" I asked. Pushing them to extend their thinking, I introduced the concepts of individualism and self-reliance.

"Does this mean farmers can do as they please?" someone asked.

"No, they are constrained by the weather and the growing season," I conjectured.

Returning to their initial impressions of their county, I asked them now to describe what values they had interjected into their community images.

"The cotton field means purity to me," voiced the creator.

"The barn represents strength, standing tall," came another reply.

"Yes," I said, nodding. "Those are all positive images. This must be a great place to live." I complimented them.

They all agreed.

I told them this was my first visit to Burke County and I had a very different impression of it than the one they had just shared with me. The students all seemed puzzled.

"What do you mean?" someone asked.

"When I was driving to your school this morning, I saw a group of twelve black parolees picking up trash off the side of the road just as I passed the Burke County line," I told them.

"There must be a lot of crime in this county," I continued in a serious tone.

Immediately there was a collective response.

"That's not true, our county isn't like that!" they called out.

"The problem for you," I said, "is to create an image of your county that fairly represents it." With this discussion I was able to introduce the Social Realists.

"These painters are trying to show us the difference between the ideals in society—democratic ideals—and the way life turned out for many people." The students were quick to see the paradox in Seymour Fogel's ink sketch titled *Negro Section, Washington, DC*. It shows a group of African Americans sitting on a front stoop, while above the roofline of their tenement, the Capitol dome clearly shines. "The dome represents American ideals—equal opportunity—and yet, what we see is a group of unemployed people," I pointed out.

After I had shown all the Regionalist and Social Realist slides and felt they could identify each genre, I asked them to vote on which genre they liked best. Regionalist won by an overwhelming majority. This did not surprise me. I think most of us are more content with romantic images because we don't have to confront the realities that are painful to think about.

The final set of slides contained examples of Public Art that the New Deal created. Optimism and hope were expressed in these works. Historical events, Americans working together, and commercial enterprises were shown in a genre I call American Idealism (Fogel and Stevens 1998). In addition, I showed the students several murals that were rejected because they did not conform to the principles of the FAP.

Studying Public Art of the 1930s serves two purposes: (1) it teaches students the history of the Great Depression and (2) it provides models for the images they will create for their own community.

Activity: Create a Mural

Students follow the same guidelines as the New Deal Artists when they plan and create a mural which reflects their community. Their mural must contain the following elements:

1. It must reflect a historic or commercial enterprise (for example, Ellis Island–New York City, Golden Gate Bridge–San Francisco, or The Alamo–San Antonio).
2. It must express hope and optimism.
3. It must not attract controversy.

Students need to organize into cooperative groups with specific responsibilities. The size of the mural depends upon how much time you can devote to the activity. If the mural is part of a unit on the Great Depression it can be as large as eight feet by twelve feet, and will require a lot of planning, research, and painting. On the other hand, an eight and a half by eleven inch single-sided sheet paper would serve for part of a lesson.

Activity: Create a Brochure

During the past decade, a significant demographic shift has occurred in the United States. Many people are leaving the "frost belt" for the Sun Belt. In addition, Silicone Valley has become the "chip" capital of the world. As of this writing, the energy crisis in California has prompted many technology firms to consider relocating to other parts of the country. Where will these firms go? And how will communities throughout the United States lure them to other regions? What factors do businesses and people consider when they have to relocate? These questions provide a framework for your students to create brochures advertising their community as a good place to live and work.

First, students should generate a list of factors that they would consider if they had to relocate. For example:

Climate

Schools

Culture

Quality of life

Sports teams

Taxes

Next, cooperative groups are assigned to investigate each of these factors. Once the research is complete, students transform their data into colorful brochures. In the process of creating the brochure, they are engaged in research and creativity.

Creating a community image is an excellent culminating activity after a unit of study on your community. It integrates all the knowledge your students have gained through their investigation and synthesizes it into a creative product. It is truly a higher-level thinking activity and one that students take pride in.

References

Bernard, R. M., and B. R. Rice. 1983. *Sunbelt Cities: Politics and Growth Since World War II.* Austin: University of Texas Press.

Bernard, R. M. 1990. *Snowbelt Cities.* Bloomington and Indianapolis: Indiana University Press.

Bustard, B. I. 1999. *One Hundred Years of Photography from the National Archives.* Washington, D.C.: National Archives and Records Adninistration in Association with the University of Washington Press Seattle and London.

Fogel, J. A. and R. L. Stevens. 1998. *Crying Out in Protest: The Formative Years of the Art of Seymour Fogel,* unpublished manuscript.

Hughes, R. 1997. *American Visions: The Epic History of Art in America.* New York: Alfred Knopf.

McElvaine, R. S. 1993. *Great Depression: America, 1929–1941,* New York: Times Books.

Pagano, M. A. and A. O'M Bowman. 1995. *Cityscapes and Capital: The Politics of Urban Development.* Baltimore: Johns Hopkins University Press.

Peeler, D. 1987. *Hope Among Us Yet: Social Criticism and Social Solace in the Great Depression.* Athens: Georgia University Press.

Rice, B. R. 1983. "If Dixie Were Atlanta." In *Sunbelt Cities: Politics and Growth Since World War II.* Austin: University of Texas Press.

Walkowitz, D. J. 1990. "A Tale of Two cities." In *Snowbelt Cities.* Bloomington and Indianapolis: Indiana University Press.

Chapter Ten

Order in the Court
Field Trip Liability

As I drove past the Atlantic Ocean on my way to Rye Junior High School during the last week of October, I thought to myself, "What a glorious day for a field trip." I had organized many field trips while teaching at Rye and had chaperoned many more, from walks to the cemetery, to trips to local basketball games, to as far away as Boston, Massachusetts, all without mishap, fortunately. Today's field trip was the culminating activity of my local history unit, a sixteen-mile bicycle tour through Rye. This would be an opportunity for all of my students to visit many of the sites we had studied during the previous weeks. We would visit several cemeteries (see Chapter 2), view the oldest house in town (see Chapter 4), and conduct an archeological activity. By the time the opening bell had rung, eighty enthusiastic eighth graders and their bicycling parents were getting organized in the school's parking lot.

At exactly 8:30 A.M., we heard a police siren; a minute later, the Rye police cruiser, flashing its blue lights, turned into the school driveway and pulled to the front of the line of bicycles. I took the final attendance. "Do you all have your lunch and a water bottle?" I asked them, one more time. Excitement in anticipation of the trip rippled through the single-file line stretching to the rear of the school. Between every eight students was a parent supervisor equally excited for the trip to begin. After we checked everything one more time, it was time to leave. The police siren again wailed and the blue lights flashed as the cruiser led a serpentine line of blaze-orange flags fluttering above the riders. A tumultuous roar from the sixth and seventh graders left behind completed our send-off.

125

We quickly peddled to Center Hill, site of the original town hall and the Congregational Church. On this spot in 1812, local residents were terrified by a British gunboat sailing toward the harbor. They evacuated the women and children safely to a neighboring town, New Market, and the militia rushed to the harbor, fired a volley, and watched the gunboat turn out to sea. We whizzed down the same hill. In a short time we had all arrived at Rye Harbor. Tied to one of the docks was a gundalow, a workboat used from Colonial times to the early 1900s. A large, single mast rose from the deck. A lanteen sail enabled the boat to sail up and down the Piscataqua River ferrying cordwood, bricks, and supplies to the other settlements on Great Bay. Alex Herlihey, president of the Gundalow Association, and a middle grades teacher at Oyster River Middle School in Durham, New Hampshire, was waiting for us on the deck. He often spoke to my classes about the role of the gundalow in local history. Today, my students would have the opportunity to tour the gundalow.

From the harbor we continued our journey to the site of the Brackett Lane massacre. In 1690, fourteen settlers were killed or captured for ransom and marched to Canada. The original graveyard at this site bears witness to their tragedy. After I gave a short narration illuminating the events of the massacre, we were back on our bikes. Following Route 1-A North, we all headed for our lunch break at Odiorne Point, the original settlement in New Hampshire.

A light easterly breeze blew off the ocean. Out at sea, the Isles of Shoals gently rested on the horizon. Their gray ledges lay low like whales in the water. "Those are Smith Isles," yelled one of the students, intending to impress his classmates with his new knowledge. Smith did in fact name the islands after himself. "Yeah, but the murders took place out there, too," another added. On the night of March 5, 1873, two Norwegian women were axe-murdered and a third escaped to accuse a Prussian immigrant of the crime. The students were well acquainted with the events of that terrible night. Based on circumstantial evidence, the jury convicted Louis Wagner of killing the two women, but to this day, doubt lingers (Stevens and Celebi 1997).

We arrived safely in time for lunch and a few planned activities. During the Gilded Age, several summer homes were built overlooking the Atlantic Ocean and Little Harbor. However, when Pearl Harbor was bombed in 1941, Odiorne Point was confiscated by the government for a military installation. It became part of the harbor defense complex, a series of six forts and batteries protecting the Portsmouth Naval Shipyard. The change in character of the landscape provided me an excellent opportunity to create an archeological activity for my students. Original roads, paths, foundations, gardens, stone walls, and allées from the Victorian era coexist with bunkers, newer roads, gun emplacements, and rubble from the WWII era. I wanted my students to create maps that described Odiorne Point in 1623 when it was settled, maps describing the area during the Victorian era in 1900, and maps to illustrate the changes that took place by 1942. They took notes and several photographs of the site to help them recall it for their map activities the following day.

This field trip was a success like all the others. The students returned to school excited, but more important, safe. What are our responsibilities when conducting field trips? Quite simply, the same as when we are teaching a class or supervising lunch or recess. Our primary duty is to protect our students from harm. This chapter will explain how the courts view our conduct when we take our students on field trips.

Tort

If one of our students is injured on a field trip, it is called a tort, a legal concept derived from the Latin word *tortus*, which means twisted. "The French words 'tortu' (twisted or crooked) and 'tort' (wrong) show the evolution of tort in its current legal definition" (Connors 1981, 2). Tort is an area of law that developed when a person wanted to recover damages caused by a wrongful act. For instance, if a student severed his fingers in a woodworking class because he was not properly trained in the use of the saw, he would have a reason to seek damages. "As far as educators are concerned, a tort is a civil wrong, independent of contract, that leads to student injuries (physical, mental, and reputation) or reduces the 'value' of the pupil by failing to provide quality instruction" (2).

We are only concerned with injuries arising from field trip activities. Negligence is the area of tort law that will help us develop a framework for field trip policies and standards of behavior. The courts use four standards to determine teacher negligence: (1) standard of care, (2) unreasonable risk, (3) proximate cause, and (4) actual injury.

Standard of Care

When we are responsible for students during school hours, field trips, and other school-sponsored activities, a certain amount of care is expected. This standard of care will vary between teachers and courses. Elementary school teachers have a higher standard of care because of the age of their students. Physical education, science, and vocational teachers have a higher standard of care because of the potential risks involved in their classes. Physical activity, volatile chemicals, and dangerous machinery require teachers to be far more aware of the conditions in their class settings. Although all teachers have general supervisory responsibilities, teachers conducting field trips may have a higher standard to uphold depending on the nature of the trip. A tour of a historic building implies a different standard of care than a white-water rafting trip down the Colorado River.

Unreasonable Risk

We have a responsibility not to place students in circumstances that could lead to unreasonable risks. Allowing sixth-grade students to play football against eighth-grade students in middle school is an example of placing students in circumstances of unreasonable risk. If you plan a field trip in the out-of-doors, perhaps to a historical site in a state or national park, you should survey the location first to determine if there are any areas that might be risky and therefore require extra planning on your part. For instance, just because alligators are plentiful in the Okeefenokee Swamp doesn't mean you should not consider a canoe trip there, but you might make some modifications to ensure student safety. You might consider using the motor-powered park boats, for example.

Proximate Cause

Proximate cause is an unusual legal principle. It is the relationship between our negligent conduct and the injury to the pupil. Our conduct does not have to be the direct cause of the injury or even the indirect cause. "It has to be the proximate—closely related in time, space, or order—cause of the injury" (Connors 1981, 8). For instance, in the Chicken Fat case, an elementary school teacher left a class that was engaged in a physical education activity unsupervised while she went to the school office. When she returned, she found a young girl crying and bleeding from the mouth. In her absence, a young boy had kicked the girl in the mouth. The girl's parents sued the school. Even though the teacher was not directly involved with the injury, lawyers argued it was the proximate cause that had resulted in the injury. If the teacher had been supervising her class, the accident would not have happened, they said. On appeal, however, the court ruled that even if the teacher were in the room, there was no guarantee that the accident would not have happened.

Actual Injury

An actual injury is any substantial physical injury. Cuts, bumps, bruises, and even broken arms that can be mended do not easily fit into this category. The injury has to require compensation. Spinal injuries, blindness, and the loss of a limb are all actual injuries—injuries arising from the negligent action of a teacher or a school district.

All four of these elements need to be present before we can be considered guilty of negligence. Following an accident, the court determines whether we have acted in a reasonable manner while exercising supervision responsibilities. This is called the reasonable man doctrine.

Reasonable Man Doctrine

The reasonable man doctrine is based on an abstract, sometimes ideal conception of how a person should behave in any given situation. Four elements determine a "reasonable person's" makeup: intelligence, physical capability of fulfilling our assignments, possession of memory, and training for the specific activities we are responsible for. The courts expect teachers in physical education, science, and vocational training to be skilled in their respective disciplines. Linked to the concept of "reasonable man" is the concept of "foreseeability." If we could have, or should have, foreseen or anticipated an accident, the failure to do so may be ruled as "negligence" (Shoop and Dunklee 1992, 266). However, the courts do not expect us to be able to see everything that will happen in the immediate future, nor do courts require us to completely ensure the safety of students. Nonetheless, they do expect us to act in a reasonable manner. If we notice defective equipment on a bus that our students are boarding for a field trip, we have a duty to bring it to the attention of the bus driver. If, on the other hand, a bus accident occurred because of faulty brake linings, we could not have reasonably foreseen the problem. All of us assume buses are in proper condition when transporting students. In one case, two teachers in Chicago organized a field trip to the city's natural history museum. The students were able to view the exhibits at the museum without direct supervision. Roberto Mancha, a student, was beaten by several boys not connected with the school. His parents sued, claiming the teachers had been negligent in their supervision. The Illinois court ruled in favor of the teachers, stating that the risk of a twelve-year-old boy being assaulted in a museum was "minimal." If teachers were forced to maintain constant supervision, the burden would be so heavy as to discourage teachers from planning educational, meaningful field trips in the future. "Moreover, the judge noted that the museum in this case had been a 'great educational enterprise,' not a place of danger" (Fischer, Schimmel, and Kelley 1991, 59).

Teachers who are teaching out of field, particularly in fields where additional training is required, leave themselves at risk. If administrators assign unqualified personnel to conduct an activity, the administrators may be held liable. The courts have created three categories of teacher responsibility based on the age of their students: (1) Children between one and seven have no capacity for negligence. The burden of supervision rests squarely on the shoulders of the supervisor. (2) For children between seven and fourteen, there can be a prima facie case of incapability. The younger the age, the greater degree of supervision is required. (3) Children between fourteen and twenty-one are presumed to be capable of being negligent.

The value of field trips cannot be overstated. A well-planned trip with proper instruction prior to the experience and followed by a culminating activity offers our students insights and perspectives they cannot receive in a traditional setting. Liability concerns should not prevent you from planning field trips. Supervision is no different than teaching in the classroom. However, if other factors such as school budgets, distance, and time create problems for you, read the Bellan and Scheurman chapter "Actual and Virtual Reality: Making the Most of Field Trips" in Part II (page 154).

References

Connors, E. T. 1981. *Educational Tort Liability and Malpractice.* Bloomington, IN: Phi Delta Kappa.

Fischer, L., D. Schimmel, and C. Kelley. 1991. *Teachers and the Law.* New York: Longman.

Liebee, H. C. 1965. *Tort Liabilities for Injuries to Pupils.* Ann Arbor, MI: Campus.

Restatement of the Law Second Torts 2d. 1991. St. Paul, MN: American Law Institute Publishers.

Shoop, R. J., and D. R. Dunklee. 1992. *School Law for the Principal: A Handbook for Practitioners.* Boston: Allyn and Bacon.

Stevens, R. L., and J. A. Celebi. 1997. *Murder at Smuttynose: An Integrated Critical Thinking Activity,* unpublished manuscript.

PART II

This section presents successful local history projects at both the middle and the secondary levels. Drawn from a national sample, each project has won either a national or a state award for excellence, or its author has been published in *Social Education*, the professional journal for the social studies. These examples of best practice reflect the commitment and creativity of social studies teachers interested in making local history come alive for their students. What I find particularly remarkable about these projects is the infinite number of possibilities they suggest for teachers interested in creating local history lessons, units, and activities. Like the study of local history, each project is tailored to meet the educational needs of students as they embark on that wonderful odyssey of learning about their community's past, present, and future. In this section, I want to mirror Michael Simpson's sentiments in his essay "Teaching History Creatively" when he states, "I am fortunate enough to feature contributors who have devoted a great deal of thought to how teachers can go beyond the limitations of lectures by actively involving their classes in the excitement of investigating the past" (in *Social Education* 1995, 3).

Chapter Eleven

A Walk Through Time
A Living History Project

Alice Aud, Gini Bland,
Barbara Brown, and Bruce Law

In the spring of 1993, students in a Georgia middle school reconstructed a Mississippian village site in an outdoor classroom on the shores of Carolina Bay. The effort was part of their study of Georgia history in eighth grade. This experience was so successful that it was repeated in social studies classes over the next two years. Because the project involved students in preparing research papers and presenting them orally in class, language arts came on board during the fourth year. These teachers were interested in broadening the project to include the frontier era.

When Screven County Middle School moved to a new campus in 1997, the project expanded to cover a six-acre site that included both the Indian village and a new frontier settlement. It was also restructured to allow students and visitors to move through its various components in chronological order. The project was accordingly renamed A Walk Through Time.

A Walk Through Time has now evolved into a student-created living history event that attracts large numbers of schoolchildren and other visitors on tour days. It begins with a walk through the woods to an archaeological dig and proceeds through Paleo, Archaic, Woodland, and Mississippian Indian sites that include an earth lodge and a replica of the Rock Eagle effigy mound. Visitors then walk through villages representing the Creek, Seminole, and Cherokee Nations by way of a gold mine that helped cause the removal of these proud peoples from their homeland. Guests join the Indians on their march along the Trail of Tears before entering the frontier settlement, where many aspects of Georgia's pioneer lifestyle are demonstrated. These include cooking; the crafts of shingle making, candle making, and hide tanning; and a blacksmith shop and a livery stable. A school, a log cabin, and law-and-order stocks on the town square are also showcased. This very serious project is also a great deal of fun!

The Project

A Walk Through Time is an interdisciplinary project that focuses on two areas of the curriculum: social studies and language arts. Social studies teachers provide the historical backdrop for the research projects that students carry out in their language arts classes. This research culminates in one long paper and at least three additional essays and speeches. It also provides the foundation for hands-on work at the site as students build historical structures and demonstrate what they have learned.

History sometimes makes little sense to middle school students because of their limited knowledge of life. The concept of having to construct homes with few or no tools in adverse conditions may not mean much until they experience it for themselves. Understanding how different groups of Native Americans lived is much easier when one is elbow deep in red clay making pots or sinking in muddy ground while sealing the sides of a sweathouse. The skills possessed by the first Americans are never more clearly evident than when students try to scrape and tan deer hides or build an earth lodge in early winter.

A Walk Through Time meets the needs of tactile/kinesthetic adolescent learners and motivates them to produce better writing as they make real connections with history. Research for an exhibit may take as long as a month, while the actual construction generally takes two or three weeks, depending on the size and complexity of the particular experience. The final step is for students to do a demonstration/presentation for visitors to the site.

The equipment needed for building an exhibit varies according to the topic chosen. Basket weaving, candle making, cooking, gardening, and growing herbs are low-budget activities. Projects such as building an earth lodge, housing and caring for farm animals, and making weapons require more money and supervision. The local 4-H club works closely with students who are working with animals. Members of the fire department are on campus during cooking and candle-making demonstrations.

As pointed out earlier, A Walk Through Time involves a close interweaving of the social studies and language arts curricula. But the project goes further to include other disciplines. For example, math teachers ask their students to calculate the area of and materials required for building a log cabin or a smokehouse. Science teachers have used the village's new sugarcane field to illustrate biological processes and our arboretum to teach students to identify native trees. Science is also part of the research for everything from diseases and medicine to making dye from walnuts and soap from lye and lard. Students in art classes create maps and graphics used in the village and the settlement, while costumes are designed and made through the support of the family living exploratory lab. Technical education students are part of the safety team and the video crew, while music remains a specific research area.

To date, the project has involved all students in the sixth and eighth grades but only one team of seventh graders. Our ultimate goal is to involve all students and all academic disciplines in this living history event. Future plans include a model farm with animal- and tractor-powered sections separated by a railroad track and a depot, a greenhouse (complete with a hydroponics system), and raised beds to be developed by seventh-grade students. The sixth grade will be responsible for the arboretum, an orchard, and a forestry plot established near the front of the grounds. Proposed agricultural products include cotton, corn, timber, and livestock, with an exhibit tracing the historical development of these commodities from earliest times to the present.

Because we are a rural county, our focus is on agriculture. However, A Walk Through Time could be centered on many other aspects of culture. A similar time line could be developed around music or dance, clothing or cooking. It could result in an architectural exhibit ranging from Old and New World pyramids to the Great Wall of China.

Assessment

A Walk Through Time addresses many of the objectives for middle school learning established by the state of Georgia. However, other project outcomes are not measurable on standard evaluative instruments. Among the results that can be documented, our students have shown an increase in writing and history scores on standardized tests as well as greater interest and higher grades in these content areas. There has also been an increase in community and parental participation and a decrease in absenteeism and discipline referrals.

As evidence of the improvement in writing skills attributed to the project, average scores from the Georgia Curriculum Based Assessment Writing Test were recorded from 1993 through 1998. When compared to other schools in our demographic group, students scored lower each year until the inclusion of the language arts component of the project in 1996. Scores in 1997 and 1998 showed steady improvement, in both cases equalling or surpassing the other schools in our group.

A Walk Through Time addresses all of the character qualities identified by the State Assembly as important for public school students. Such characteristics as good citizenship, cooperation, self-control, compassion, creativity, and respect for the environment take on new meaning when experienced in the setting of a community that students adopt as their own. It is difficult to put a quantifiable grade on the skills learned through working in a group setting and being accountable to others, but these vital attributes are critical to the future of our students.

"Just plain fun" is also part of this experience, and the obvious pleasure in learning and doing is as easy to identify as it is difficult to formally evaluate. Some students discover a gift for teaching younger children, others uncover an interest in cooking or woodworking, and still others develop a simple love of the outdoors. This experience can also call forth unsuspected talents; one student with an intellectual disability and a speech impediment gave a remarkable performance, which he repeated over and over to groups visiting the site.

Even though Screven County is rural, most of our students have almost no firsthand experience in an agricultural setting. Participating in or visiting the site of A Walk Through Time corrects a lot of misconceptions. Two years ago, a kindergarten child asked whether "that great big bull laid eggs," her only experience with this concept having been the eggs sitting next to the milk in the grocery store.

In sum, the effects of this project are assessed continually in both traditional and nontraditional ways. All students are evaluated on their understanding of core knowledge and standard research methods through written tests and the research paper. Other skills are measured on an ongoing basis as students work on the construction site. Safety skills are taught to all students before they are allowed to enter the site. Upon completion of the project, student attitudes are measured through a written evaluation in the form of a questionnaire, a survey, or an informal essay.

The School and the Community

School systems are reflections of the communities they serve. Screven County Middle School in Sylvania is the only middle school in this county of some 14,000 people. The population is made up largely of blue-collar working-class people. The school population of 714 students in three grades is 57 percent African American and 43 percent Anglo-American, with 14 percent of students enrolled in a special education program.

Improved ties between the middle school and the community have been an important outgrowth of the Walk Through Time project. Parents and other community members are proud of the innovative achievements of their middle school students. They offer various kinds of help to the project, often coming in after school and on Saturdays during the construction phase of the project. Last spring, a neighbor assisted with the planting of the first sugarcane crop, and he has agreed to help with the harvesting and syrup boiling in the fall. A local farmer has put a wagon (circa 1880) on permanent loan in our frontier site. A blacksmith and other reenactors often join us for the tour days.

Some three thousand people visit A Walk Through Time on tour days. Students from the local elementary school, with an approximate enrollment of sixteen hundred students, come on buses provided by the county. Several high school and alternative school classes also make the trip. Additionally, seven other schools outside of our county visited on tour days last spring.

Conclusion

A Walk Through Time is an innovative idea that crosses all academic disciplines and developmental boundaries among students. It addresses the goal of high academic achievement through both traditional assignments and direct hands-on experience in carrying out projects.

For schools wishing to replicate this idea, the physical site of a school will largely determine the extent of the project. Although an open field or a wooded site is ideal, parts of this activity can be carried out in a school parking lot. Basic skills and crafts require minimal funding, while major construction activities obviously call for more resources. We are now developing a curriculum guide that will include not only a large variety of topics for exploration but also variations on the presentation of each topic.[1]

The majority of students who have participated in this project over the past seven years recall the "Indian Village" as the high point of their middle school experience. We believe A Walk Through Time exemplifies the conditions for ideal learning proposed by John Dewey and elaborated on in Dan Rea's model of serious fun in social studies.

Notes

Alice Aud, Gini Bland, Barbara Brown, and Bruce Law are middle grade teachers at Screven County Middle School in Sylvania, Georgia.

1. To find out more about how to adapt this project, write to the Innovation Program of the Georgia Department of Education, 1852 Twin Towers East, Atlanta, GA 30334; or call Brendan Long at (404) 657-8335.

Chapter Twelve

Old Hometown

Melinda Beckett

Old Hometown is a heritage-based service learning program of the School District of Escambia County in partnership with the Historic Pensacola Preservation Board. It began six years ago as a summer program for Pensacola High School students. Old Hometown became a magnet program open to all area high school students with at least a 2.5 GPA and good conduct records in 1996. At that time, Old Hometown moved into a historic house donated by the Historic Pensacola Preservation Board.

For two years, in addition to high school students, more than one hundred middle school students from the PATS (Program for Academically Talented Students) Center attended Old Hometown two days per week, along with two teachers. Many eighth graders plan to return to Old Hometown during their tenth-grade year. We are a very unique, innovative program and currently the only magnet service learning program in Florida!

The primary purpose of Old Hometown is to promote an awareness of the history of Pensacola while teaching students how to use technology. Pensacola is the place of the first European settlement in what is now the United States, preceding St. Augustine and Plymouth Rock. Students work with T. T. Wentworth State Museum personnel, research the rich historical records of our community, interview senior citizens, and create publications, dramatic presentations, and puppet shows that reflect this research. The products of student research utilize technology in all forms. For example, interviews with senior citizens are photographed, video- and audiotaped, and transcribed through word processing via our computer lab. Additional research is conducted through Internet sources that provide access to archival materials. Students serve

Figure 1

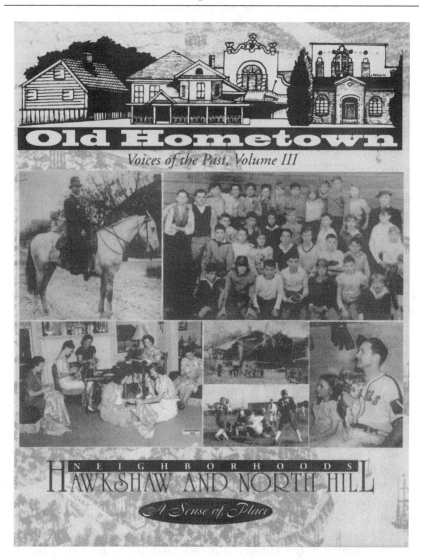

as living history interpreters, job shadow in occupations such as plane restoration and historical architecture, and work in historic restoration. Since all student work is real work with measurable products, the students learn how to use technology as it is used in real-life situations. Using a software program to plan an actual restoration is more meaningful than using the same program to complete a worksheet. Contracts are prepared by the students and the teachers at the beginning of the grading period. Each student selects areas of concentration and service learning projects. At the end of the marking period, each student must document his or her learning through logs, essays, oral and written exams, and performance-based portfolios to account for the grades. This has proven to be very successful and rewarding for the teachers and the students.

A unique problem of Florida is that most people who live in Florida are not natives of our state. Old Hometown students, by creating many opportunities for people in our community to learn our history, are helping promote stewardship and citizenship among all community members. Our main project is the annual oral history publication titled *Voices of the Past*. We are currently working on our sixth volume, *Pensacola Remembers the 20th Century*. This is the students' tribute to the millennium.

Last year our living history presentation for the National History Day Competition was based on the theme of conflict in the '50s and the '60s using Pensacola's replica of the Wall Memorial, Wall South, as the backdrop. The 1997 history fair project, titled "Jonathan Walker, The Man with the Branded Hand," which won first place in district and state competitions and placed eleventh in the nation, won Best of Show in Florida during the National History Day Competition in Washington, D.C.

Students have also written and produced historical plays, coloring books, museum catalogs, newspaper supplements, video documentaries, and puppet shows for younger students. The purpose of the historical puppet play is to teach Pensacola history while reinforcing reading skills. *Pensacola, Where America Began* is about the DeLuna landing in the area and emphasizes the many groups of people who came to Pensacola. This play is performed at elementary schools in Pensacola and includes prereading and postreading activities.

In addition, Old Hometown students participate in service learning by serving as tour guides for elementary students who visit the Historic Pensacola Village, Colonial Kidstown, a section of the T. T. Wentworth State Museum, and acting as the official guides for public tours of the restored houses in the village. Students provide these services dressed in period costumes, mainly from the 1800s. Service learning is multifaceted and fun at Old Hometown!

Finally, we were honored to be recognized as a nominee for the National Service Learning Leader School. We have been recognized for our accomplishments by Columbia and Florida Scholastic Press, the National Freedoms Foundation, the Sunshine State Public Relations Association, and other state and local organizations. The University of West Florida has placed four student teachers here and Pensacola

Junior College has supported us with coordination of our program and its dual enrollment program. With a 98 percent return rate by our students, we feel we have created a program that has something for just about everyone. As former Old Hometown student Noah Shelton concluded,

> "During the first half of the school year I have done things that I would have never expected to do before. I have learned and digested knowledge of historic happenings in Pensacola, and all of this learning I have done willingly. Old Hometown's method of 'doing is learning' has taken this student hook, line, and sinker. Although not earth shattering, the concept of Old Hometown is one that is radically unique. Not only does it strengthen the bonds students have with the community, it serves to preserve local history by keeping the memories strong in the minds of the current generation."

Note

Melinda Beckett is a teacher with Old Hometown, a heritage-based service learning program of the Escambia County School District, Pensacola, Florida.

Hawkshaw and North Hill: A Sense of Place
from Old Hometown 1996–1997: Neighborhoods

Erica Enfinger

For most of the school children of the North Hill and Hawkshaw area, the mode of transportation to school was walking or riding a bike. Henry Anson of North Hill recalls, "School buses were only in the rural areas." He further explains, "There was no bus system for the children who lived in the city."

Diane Crona of North Hill remembers, "The school buses were reserved just for what we considered the real rural students." The children had to find their way to school rain or shine. When asked what the school children had to do when it was raining, Adalia Berry Schwab responds, "Really, we got wet. Our mamas had no excuse. We had to go to school. But we loved every minute of it."

Because it was a time of segregation, white children in Hawkshaw attended Eliza Jane Wilson Elementary School, while black children attended A. M. DeVaughn Elementary School. Addie June Hall recalls the confusion she felt about the schooling arrangements as a child. She had a best friend who spent most of her spare time in Ms. Hall's home. The girl often even slept in the same bed as Ms. Hall, but because the girl was white, she and Addie June Hall had to attend separate schools. "She had to go to that school [Eliza Jane Wilson] and I had to go to A. M. DeVaughn, and we could not understand how come we had to go to different schools," Ms. Hall recalls, "Most children of North Hill attended P. K. Yonge." Parents in North Hill and Hawkshaw who chose to send their children to private schools often chose St. Michael's Catholic School.

Kindergarten was not a requirement for children at this time. Any kindergarten classes conducted in the Pensacola area were not in the public schools. Jane Seligman of North Hill recalls her kindergarten experiences in Ms. Elsie's Kindergarten: "She had the first kindergarten in Pensacola." She further explains, "Her first place was down on Spring and Gregory Streets and she had a room in her house. . . . Nearly everybody in Pensacola went to Ms. Elsie's Kindergarten."

The majority of children started school in the first grade at the age of six. Most of the interviewees recall their elementary school experiences as positive. Addie June Hall remembers of A. M. DeVaughn, "We received, at that time, all the hand-downs from all of the other schools. We had the wooden desks; nothing new—never, never had anything new." She further explains, "But we had some good strong teachers there and I'm so glad of that. Teachers who taught us to write. I don't recall anybody in our classroom not being able to read. Everybody had to read. You read. You knew your tables." She goes on to explain that the teachers at A. M. DeVaughn prepared the students well for life in the outside world. Harry Kahn of North Hill remembers his elementary school years fondly as well. "I went to P. K. Yonge school for eight years. Enjoyed nearly every minute of it," he reminisces. Adalia Berry Schwab of Hawkshaw recalls her experiences at Eliza Jane Wilson, "Oh yes! It was a very good school. We were real disciplined. We learned an awful lot. We had wonderful teachers." She continues, "All of them were my favorites."

Most of the residents of Hawkshaw and North Hill we interviewed considered schooling today very different from their schooling, especially in the area of discipline. The general opinion was that proper discipline was considered far more important in their day than it is today. This belief applied to schools both public and private; students at that time were required to behave better than students today. Henry Anson of North Hill describes the nuns at St. Michael's Catholic School as being "very strict disciplinarians." He goes on to explain, "If you got to fooling around there, you would get your hand whacked with a ruler." Jane Seligman of North Hill fondly remembers, "I had a wonderful English teacher. She really drilled us. Oh! She was strict, but oh, she drilled us." She goes on to explain that she now notices the incorrect grammar on television and radio because of the strict teaching. Diane

Crona of North Hill says in comparing the disciplinary standards of yesterday and today, "they [the teachers] were strict. Some of the things that I understand that go on in classrooms today, I mean, would have been totally unheard of. They would have been out of school so fast, they wouldn't have known what hit 'em. . . . Things were so close knit, and there was so much more interaction with teachers and parents. They [the teachers] would not think twice about calling a parent, nor would a parent think two times about calling your teacher."

Richard Zelius of North Hill recalls disciplinary measures at his school as "Embarrassment was the worst punishment—to be called dumb. . . ." Most of the interviewees agreed that the stricter discipline in their schools led to a better learning environment than that of today.

Junior high schools of the day included A. V. Clubbs School, J. B. Lockee (changed to W. A. Blount in the '40s), and W. A. Blanchard. St. Michael's Catholic and P. K. Yonge schools also ran through the junior high years. Though most of the interviewees did not seem to recall as much of their junior high years as they did of their elementary school and high school years, the junior high years were still important.

According to our interviewees, students often dropped out of school during their junior high or high school years. This happened in both North Hill and Hawkshaw. By the time some of these kids were fifteen or sixteen, they had to devote their time to working and supporting their families. This practice was especially common during the Depression years. Many of our interviewees told us that young women were often married at the age of sixteen, seventeen, or eighteen and chose to devote their time to starting a family instead. Many students just believed that more opportunities awaited them outside of school. Some had family businesses that they had to help run and truly had no need for further education. Richard Zelius of North Hill remembers that he opted to finish his high school education through night school and got a job driving a Coca-Cola truck in the daytime instead.

Most of those interviewed have many fond memories of their high schools as well. Years ago there were only three high schools in the Hawkshaw and North Hill areas. These schools were segregated until the 1960s. Whites in the area attended Pensacola High School and African Americans attended Booker T. Washington High School (officially it was only Washington High School until the early '40s). Those who chose to attend private school went to Catholic High School.

Many of our interviewees attended Pensacola High School when the building, which was completed in 1922, was located on the east side of Lee Square on North Palafox Street. According to the *Pensacola Sunday News*, the structure of Pensacola High School east of Lee Square cost $300,000.00. It was said to be the finest school building in the state of Florida at the time.

Pensacola High School was the largest high school in the area. Eugene Elebash of North Hill remembers that even though the building was made to accommodate only approximately 800 students, in the late '30s it housed, according to Elebash, around "1,200 to 1,400 students"; the Pensacola High School class of 1938 had 275 graduates. In comparison, Catholic High School had "10 to 15" graduates per year. Washington High School was located on Jackson and C Streets, then A and Strong Streets, and later on Texar Drive where the J. E. Hall Center is today. In 1940, there were 409 students enrolled at Washington High School.

Besides the basic "Readin', Writin', and 'Rithmetic," high school was also the center of most students' social lives. Diane Crona of North Hill explains, "There were only three high schools in Pensacola. There were PHS, Catholic, and Washington, and that was it! So you knew everybody that was in that school." She talks about the popularity of high school dances and how many people attended the dances. Social life revolved around school. Crona explains, "High school clubs were real big and real important and everybody belonged to something, just depending on what your interests were."

Until recent years, a college education was not necessary to be successful. Women often married after high school and took care of the children at home, and that was expected of them. Some women went on to normal schools, where they trained to become teachers: their way of serving the community. There were women who chose other careers. Sybil Dedmond of Hawkshaw decided when she was young that she wanted to be a lawyer and attended Howard University. She majored in political science and psychology and continued her studies at the University of Chicago. About her decision to pursue a career outside of what were considered traditional fields for women, Sybil Dedmond says, "I always intended to be a lawyer and I decided that was the route I wanted to take early partly because I wanted to do something about what I considered injustices at the time and do something about helping bring about some change." Men in the North Hill and Hawkshaw area also took many different paths following high school. Some went to work with their families or took on other jobs that did not require a college education. Many joined the military, which was quite a respected field. At this time many women wanted to marry military officers because they made better money, according to some, than men in most other areas of work. Other men did go to college to enter professional fields. Brent Watson says about the University of Florida, "When I was down there, we had 2,500 students." Today, the student population of the University of Florida is around 40,000 students. Women attended FSU in Tallahassee, which was at that time a women's school.

No matter what path a student in North Hill or Hawkshaw took in his education, he still considered basic education important. Though many students in the two neighborhoods did not complete their high school education, they remember the important basics they learned during their school years. Those who were fortunate enough to complete high school and attend college learned to appreciate education that much more. Today, these citizens try to instill the importance of education in their children and grandchildren.

Chapter Thirteen

The Real World
Community Speakers in the Classroom
Lindy G. Poling

Since I was a child, I have loved the study of history, but as a young teacher, I quickly discovered that not all of my students shared my passion. So I began experimenting with different methods to make the learning of history more inviting. One of the most successful methods has been inviting guest speakers—veterans, elected officials, businesspeople, authors, and parents—into the classroom. Guest speakers can motivate students to think more critically about their lessons, challenge them with inquiring questions, and affirm the importance of citizenship and good character. Speakers from the community also provide stories and personal perspectives that make the curriculum more interesting and understandable.[1] In this article, I will explain how the Community-in-the-Classroom (CIC) program works and describe the positive effects of CIC on student learning and character development.

Experiential Learning

Real-world examples can make the study of science, math, and social studies more inviting. Experiential learning is gaining favor across a number of disciplines as an effective way to organize curriculum and instruct students. For example, a large teacher-training program was initiated in 1999 in the Durham, North Carolina, public schools to help math teachers "bring numbers to life" using experiential instructional methods. "If we can tie the mathematical idea to their own experience, [students will be] more likely to remember it," commented Durham math teacher Steve Unruhe.[2] He uses measures of cholesterol content of various fast-food meals as data when he teaches statistical concepts such as mean and median. The Scientist-in-the-Classroom program, under way in several counties in North Carolina, promotes the use of scientists, engineers, mathematicians, and other professionals as guest speakers.[3]

Why not use experiential learning in social studies classes? For more than two decades, I have investigated the benefits of experiential learning in my American history classes. I have found that not only are experiential instructional methods more stimulating, but they also help students become better critical thinkers. Students are challenged to think critically about major historical themes through special readings, classroom discussions, enlightening videos, and team-based research projects. As they delve into their chosen topics, I stress the need to gather complete information and to let facts guide their thinking, not emotion or conjecture. The fruits of each student or group inquiry are shared by all through classroom presentations. Toward the end of a unit of study, community speakers join each class to give their special insight into a historical period, an event, or a societal issue (see information on page 153, *Best Practices in a Community-in-the-Classroom*).

Preparation

Before having someone speak in your class, do some preliminary screening. This is especially important when someone volunteers his or her services without having been trained or sponsored by an organization you know. Discuss the person's background as it relates to the subject area and whether he or she has previously addressed a school audience. If the person is unknown to you, it is appropriate to ask for a resume and a personal reference. Perhaps your school has a staff member, such as a career development coordinator, who can help you recruit effective guest speakers. Many civic organizations like the nonpartisan League of Women Voters have recommended guest speakers or could help lead you to them.[4]

Identify classroom objectives and inform a speaker about what students have been studying relating to this topic and how long the presentation should be, including at least fifteen minutes for questions and answers. Assure the speaker that students and teachers will have carefully prepared questions as well as spontaneous questions. If your school district is making special efforts to teach important character traits, let the speaker know which traits are being emphasized (for example, respect, responsibility, kindness, good judgment, courage, and perseverance).

If your principal is wary of having a guest speaker address a sensitive topic, explain how you have prepared the class for critical analysis and familiarized your speaker with the classroom policy. Point out that the speaker is only one element of the materials your class will consider. Mention your careful question-and-answer plans. Be ready to consider inviting a second speaker who can offer a different point of view. In some schools, an administrator will occasionally sit in on classes with guest speakers.[5]

Students can begin preparing for a guest speaker months in advance. Those who view history as useless may feel spurred to apply themselves when they know that a guest speaker will be featured near the end of the unit of study. If the students have some familiarity with the topic to be covered by the speaker, they will be prepared to ask intelligent questions—and to weigh the speaker's answers against other sources of information.

As the day draws near, give students an outline of what will happen and carefully explain how you would like the question-and-answer session to proceed. Give students a background sheet on the invited speaker, which could include a brief biography and source of expertise. Students should prepare questions that can be reviewed by the teacher and, possibly, forwarded to the speaker ahead of time. Return these questions to the students just before the visitor arrives. This allows students to feel more comfortable asking questions in class. Spontaneous questions can also be encouraged.

Good Morning, Vietnam

Students who view history as boring will be disarmed by the experience of having a Vietnam veteran like Carl Bimbo share pictures of his lost buddies with the class.[6] The Vietnam era is a bad memory for many Americans, but for this veteran and many others, there are important experiences that should not be forgotten. Although there may be disagreement over the lessons to be learned from that war, a study of the era can encourage students to reflect on their own convictions and to become aware of the political and moral dimensions of foreign policy.[7] In essence, Carl Bimbo helps students better comprehend the true costs of war.

Brigadier General George B. Price has traveled all the way from Columbia, Maryland, to spend a full day with my students. He shows

Figure 1

that we can discuss a controversial topic like the Vietnam era with respect and dignity, and he emphasizes how vital it is for each of us to participate in the democratic process. A veteran of the Korean and Vietnam Wars, General Price delivers the message that we live in a peaceful and prosperous land because of the ultimate sacrifice that so many American men and women have made to preserve our liberty and freedom.

In his presentation, General Price brings us into his world, explaining why he was willing to risk his life, and the lives of his soldiers, for his country. He challenges all of us to rethink generalizations we may believe relating to Vietnam. My students, visiting parents, and teachers were particularly moved when he stopped for a moment, looked at the audience, and said, "Your challenge as Americans is to find the profits of peace." One student wrote, "General Price inspired me to believe we can do anything we put our minds to by being an example of a person who grew up in a segregated Mississippi and rose to become one of the nation's outstanding Brigadier Generals through a lot of hard work and perseverance. He is a man whom the entire world could benefit to hear."

Figure 2

Law and Order

Few units of study are more difficult to teach, or more important for our students to understand, than the U.S. Constitution. Rather than relying totally on my own knowledge, I invite Assistant District Attorney Shelley Desvousges into my class to describe the Constitution and the Bill of Rights as they are applied today. By arrangement, Shelley Desvousges entertains questions that have been carefully and critically developed by each student. Exciting discussions evolve and, as a result, my students no longer view the Constitution as a document written for the 1790s, but rather one that is relevant for 2001 and beyond.

Aftermath

Having parents and community speakers come into the classroom is not only a powerful tool for bringing history to life, but it is also effective in affirming the importance of good character and good citizenship. Visits by guest speakers frequently lead to student involvement in a variety of civic-oriented and career development activities. After a recent visit by State Senator Eric Reeves, an eleventh grader wrote, "You have definitely made an impact on the way I feel about politics and law. I believe this may be my new direction as I enter college in the next couple of years." Another student commented, "You captured my interest when you discussed why you chose politics. I remember you stating it was something you always had an interest in, and you enjoyed getting involved through various projects in high school and college, such as the soup kitchen and being the Chaplain's assistant. You confirmed my thoughts that it was important to get involved."

After every guest speaker's presentation, I write a letter of thanks to the speaker. I assign students to write letters (which will be graded) that discuss what they have learned from the experience. With students' permission, I send copies of the letters to the classroom visitor. I also invite students to consider writing articles about the experience for submission to the PTA newsletter, the school paper, or the local newspaper.

Community Enthusiasm

One of the major conclusions of the report *Knowledge for a Nation of Learners: A Framework for Education Research* is that "families and communities must be more involved in education. Public schools should become, in spirit and in practice, more public."[8] Public education seems to always be in the news, and I have found a high level of community interest in supporting teachers. As Tom Oxholm, the chairperson of the Wake County Business-Education Leadership Council (BELC) commented, "We are just waiting for the teachers to tell us what to do!"

I have been pleasantly surprised that busy professionals will devote half a day or more to talking with students. Community members and parents are more than willing to support teachers with their time and other resources. For my popular elective course The Lessons of Vietnam, parents, community members, and the Millbrook High School PTA have furnished books, video collections, and even funding that made it possible for me to participate in an educational study tour of Vietnam.[9]

There is another benefit of getting the community into the classroom. By linking community members directly with students and teachers, they become more understanding of the problems educators face. They might see crowded classrooms and become more concerned about the real effects of limited school funds on the overall quality of educational resources and programs.

Conclusion

By bringing well-informed guest speakers from the community into the classroom, we can encourage our students to assess multiple points of view and to think more creatively and critically about their coursework. The questions that they prepare in advance, as well as the classroom discussions and follow-up reflective writings, promote higher-order critical-thinking skills. And the social studies content students learn no longer seems like just schooling; it is part of the real world.

Notes

Linda G. Poling is a social studies teacher at Millbrook High School in Raleigh, North Carolina. E-mail: lgpoling@juno.com.

1. Stephen A. Janger, "Civic Apathy: Who Cares?" *Education Week* (18 March 1998) (www.edweek.org/ew/1998/27janger.h17); Linda Torp and Sara Sage, *Problems as Possibilities* (Alexandria, VA: Association for Supervision and Curriculum Development, 1998), 81; Olivia Baker, "Vietnam's Echoes on the Home Front," *USA Today* (20 December 1999), L2.

2. Jonathan Goldstein, "Math? No Problem!" *The News and Observer* (Raleigh, NC: 9 September 1999), 1B.

3. Laura Myers, "Education Research Must Make Lifelong Learning Its Goal, Report Says." *The News and Observer* (Raleigh, NC: 17 December 1996), 11A.

4. Find the League of Women Voters on the web at <www.lwv.org>, or call the LWV chapter in your state.

5. This section is adapted from Vietnam Veterans Memorial Fund, *Echoes from the Wall: History, Learning and Leadership Through the Lens of the Vietnam War Era* (1977), 77, which can be found at <www.teachvietnam.org> or obtained by sending a request via fax to (202) 393-0029.

6. Several organizations that provide speakers in many communities on the topic of the Vietnam War can be found on page 82 of *Echoes from the Wall.*

7. Don Bakker, *The Limits of Power: The United States in Vietnam* (Providence, RI: Brown University, 1993), ii.

8. U.S. Department of Education, *Knowledge for a Nation of Learners: A Framework for Education Research* (Washington, D.C.: USDOE, 1996).

9. I would like to thank the Wake Education Partnership for providing financial resources to develop the Best Practices Guide; the Millbrook High School PTA for its sponsorship of my travel-study program in Vietnam, "The Bridge Back"; and Wake County School Superintendent Dr. Jim Surratt, Associate Superintendent Dr. Bill McNeal, and my husband, Dr. Barclay Poling, for their support of the Community-in-the-Classroom program.

Best Practices in a Community-in-the-Classroom (CIC) Social Studies Program Guide provides details of the CIC methodology and gives practical suggestions for developing a network of community guest speakers. The guide is available free on the web at www.wcpss.net/community_in_the_classroom/ or in book form ($5.00 black and white, $34 with color) by writing to Lindy Poling, 2404 Weybridge Drive, Raleigh, NC 27615.

Chapter Fourteen

Actual and Virtual Reality
Making the Most of Field Trips

Jennifer Marie Bellan and Geoffrey Scheurman

The very mention of a field trip often makes even the most reticent students excited. Field trips can provide that rare instance when history or government comes close to being real for students. Unfortunately, most teachers have tales of field trips that ended in disaster or were fun but nearly void of educational value.

With the advent of the Internet, a popular new phenomenon in social studies classrooms is the virtual field trip. Ironically, many of the same concerns teachers express about actual field trips have their electronic counterparts. Bluntly stated, either kind of field trip can be a monumental waste of time. Figure 1 suggests five reasons that this is so.

Despite their pitfalls, there are potential strengths associated with both actual and virtual field trips. Moreover, the strengths offered by one kind of field trip may help alleviate the concerns associated with the other. Indeed, virtual and actual field trips can serve as complementary components in a powerful instructional approach.

Living in the upper Midwest, we have enjoyed the living history approach created at Ft. Snelling Historic Site in St. Paul, Minnesota. We recently discovered that the fort is depicted on a website at <http://www.mnhs.org/sites/snelling/index.html>. A cursory look at the site suggests that it is nothing more than a glorified travel brochure. But then it occurred to us that a cursory tour through the actual fort might lead an unprepared observer to believe that it, too, is nothing more than "just another history place."

Figure 1
Field Trips and Their Pitfalls.

Actual Field Trip

- Teachers use docents and other curatorial staff as temporary baby-sitters for busloads of students in search of entertainment.

- Students approach the trip like tourists and spend most of their time wandering the grounds and horsing around.

- Students are poorly prepared for the visual, verbal, or tactile lessons that await them; even the best teacher preparation erodes under the contagious excitement of a day out of school.

- Students cannot glean the intended benefit from an experience away from school because there are too many objectives in the "lesson" and the site is too overwhelming.

- The actual field trip is seen as an end in itself and there is little or no follow-up on the information gathered during the trip.

Virtual Field Trip

- Teachers use computers as baby-sitters for classrooms full of students in search of visual and auditory stimulation.

- Students approach the computer in much the same way they approach television, aimlessly surfing the web and cursorily taking in sights.

- Advance preparation seldom occurs; many teachers use the Internet as an escape from the classroom or a carrot to gain compliance from bored or disruptive students.

- Students cannot benefit from the computer because teachers view it as a font of infinite knowledge and present students with amorphous objectives such as "get information about. . ."

- The virtual field trip is seen as an end in itself and there is little or no follow-up on the information gathered during the trip.

What if we used the virtual site to help students prepare for an actual trip and to extend that trip when we were back in the classroom? Better yet, what if we tried the radical notion of using the website not as a resource to get answers about the real world, but as an instrument to write questions about it? What follows is a plan we have devised to harness students' curiosity—often unbridled, chaotic, and without direction—in such a way that both actual and virtual field trips can realize their full potential.

Constructing the World of Fort Snelling

A. Teacher does advance search of the actual site.

1. Anticipate positive student experiences at the actual fort site.
   Activities at this living history museum range from tea parties and 1820s immersion experiences to birthday parties. Advance planning to check for availability (and possible student birthdays) will help teacher field questions of "can we do that?"

2. Anticipate student frustration level during initial exploration of the actual site.
   Students will experience a vast array of buildings, constraints due to safety considerations, and museum workers who respond to their questions "in character" (as actors) or "in real life" (as docents). For some students, hypothetical thinking is difficult; therefore, they need help in preparing to ask questions.

B. Teacher does advance search of the virtual site.

1. Anticipate positive student experiences at the website.
   The site has a virtual tour, photographs, biographies, and sketches of outbuildings with basic historical information.

Figure 2

Photo by Jennifer Marie Bellan, Historic Sites Photography

2. Anticipate possible student frustration level during initial exploration of the virtual site.
   Are the graphics too big? Will it take too long to download images and text? Is the readability level appropriate?

C. Teacher determines how the website can alleviate concerns about the actual trip and vice versa.

1. As part of a three-column Pocket Portfolio (see Figure 3), the teacher prepares a virtual tour guide for students to complete while they are online.
   Students will use the information on the website to record, in their own words, what they expect to encounter at various locations within the actual fort. The teacher may ask students to retrieve simple information (When was the fort built? Who was it named after and why?), to make narrative predictions, to create drawings of various aspects of historical life (What appears to have been the role of women at the fort?), and to anticipate other aspects of the actual trip (What unique things should we look for in this part of Fort Snelling? Are there safety precautions?).

2. Students turn the Virtual Tour Guide into an Actual Tour Guide to take on the trip.
   Pocket Portfolios should include notes from the virtual trip and questions for docents and "living" historical characters based on these notes. Students leave space to compare their predictions with actual observations and to make new drawings when they visit the actual fort. They also make space for other personal reflections—for example, on smells, tactile experiences, or funny things that happen to them.

3. Students become experts on a specific location within the fort.
   Prior to the actual trip, pairs of students download sketches of a specific building and summarize notes on the nature of the activity that takes place there. These are made into placards and placed around the classroom. Students re-create the fort and take one another on an in-class tour that foreshadows the eventual trip to Fort Snelling. For example, students might anticipate their discussions with docents or historical characters by acting out hypothetical scenes at each station in the classroom. The class then helps each pair of experts think of good questions to ask on the day of the actual trip.

D. Students visit Fort Snelling using their Pocket Portfolios.

1. If a regular tour or age-appropriate program exists, students may participate in it. If not, groups of four may complete their Pocket Portfolios during a specified amount of time.
   Usually, historic sites have well-trained staff and a regular educational program. Providing educators at the site with a listing of students' questions beforehand can help them direct their "speeches" or "roles" toward those topics.

Figure 3
A Sample Page from the Pocket Portfolio.

Virtual Tour Guide	Actual Tour Guide	Follow-Up Guide
Next, you and a partner will select a single location within Fort Snelling and prepare to become experts on the functions and activity that took place there in 1823. My partner is: _____ Our area of expertise is: _____ From the website: My building looks like (sketch outside and some aspect of inside):	Make a record of your observations at Fort Snelling. Specific things you will look for (check off when found): Sketch of the actual site (one person makes sketch of outside, other makes sketch of inside):	Now you will return to the website for Fort Snelling and compare your expectations with your actual observations. What did you find that was unexpected (i.e., not on the website)? What aspect of your area was most like you expected?
		How were your sketches accurate or inaccurate?
		What was your best question (and why)?
My expectations are (smell, sights, sounds, feelings):	Questions for living historians (you may summarize your dialogue on the bus):	
		What was the best answer (and why)?
		What would you ask if you could go back again?

Figure 4

Photo by Jennifer Marie Bellan, Historic Sites Photography

2. Initial information-gathering efforts are discussed before experts proceed to their respective areas of study.

   After the official tour (or at a predetermined time), students reconvene at a designated place to share the results of their museum explorations and to get ready for their final task as experts. Partners then head for the locations they selected in class, where they interview historic characters and enter detailed drawings in their portfolios. This requires a certain degree of trust on the teacher's part, as students may scatter to all corners of the site. Parent chaperones assigned to certain clusters of students can help monitor the activity.

E. **Students bring completed Pocket Portfolios to class for discussion and evaluation.**

1. Students return to the Internet and complete the final portion of their Pocket Portfolios.

   During the initial virtual tour, students predicted and drew what they expected. At Fort Snelling, they recorded some of their actual observations and conversations. Returning to the website, they can reconsider what they expected and decide on the accuracy of their predictions.

2. Each pair of experts does a presentation on what they discovered at the fort.

Pairs may choose to conduct a brief reenactment of their interview with a living historian, debate the accuracy of history as it is presented at the fort or on the website, or other possible activities. Teachers should have a rubric for scoring presentations and providing feedback to students.

3. Students complete a final writing project and prepare to submit their Pocket Portfolios.

   Teachers may culminate the lesson with a creative writing assignment. For example, students might write two letters to the living historians they met at Fort Snelling—one in an imaginary historical role (conceived by the student or provided by the teacher) and another as a contemporary student sharing the highlights of his or her trip to the fort.

Benefits

Does the virtual field trip replace the actual site? No. On one hand, no matter how sophisticated computers become, the tactile, olfactory, visual, and dialogical experience of an actual field trip cannot be replicated from hundreds of miles away. On the other hand, artifacts and images from books and readings, and now computers, can sensitize a student's sense of touch, smell, and sight to the plethora of stimuli to be encountered at the actual site. Perhaps more important, the use of this information can help provide students with prior knowledge and questions that will enhance their conversations when they visit the actual site. Finally, just as an actual site can bring the flavor of history to the here and now, a virtual field trip can help students reach into the past in a more meaningful way.

The idea of interweaving curriculum objectives with resources on the Internet seems increasingly to be the goal of many educators. We think that using the computer for the sake of using the computer is misguided. However, if intellectual rigor, disciplinary objectives, and appropriate assessment practices are maintained, there is a place for the Internet in helping increase the authentic learning of students. What follows is a very brief listing of websites and lesson plan link sites (most created by teachers) that we have reviewed and found to serve many of the objectives described in this article.

Teaching Resources

Lesson Plans & Resources for Social Studies Teachers
<http://www.csun.edu/~hcedu013/index.html>

Resources for Teaching About the Americas
<http://ladb.unm.edu/retanet/>

Figure 5

Photo by Jennifer Marie Bellan, Historic Sites Photography

Ask Asia from The Asia Society
<http://www.askasia.org/index.htm>

Connections +
<http://www.mcrel.org/connect/plus>

Lesson Plans Page
<http://www.coe.missouri.edu/~kyle/edu.html>

Other sites that can start you on your own virtual field trip adventure:

Rock and Roll Hall of Fame
<http://www.rockhall.com>

U.S. Census Bureau
<http://www.census.gov>

World Heritage List
<http://www.unesco.org/whc/heritage.htm>

Teaching with Historic Places
<http://www.cr.nps.gov/nr/twhp/hom.html>

End of the Oregon Trail Interpretive Center
<http://www.teleport.com/~eotic/index.html>

Salem Witch Museum 1692
<http://www.salemwitchmuseum.com/>

National Geographic Society
<http://nationalgeographic.com/>

Ice Age National Scenic Trail
<http://www.nps.gov/iatr/>

Note

Jennifer Marie Bellan is currently a substitute teacher and a recent graduate with a master of arts degree in teaching history. She has had experience working as a visual information specialist for the Smithsonian Institution. Geoffrey Scheurman is associate professor of teacher education at the University of Wisconsin–River Falls. The authors would like to thank the educators and enactors at Fort Snelling for lending their costumed talents to the photographs.

Chapter Fifteen

Doing REAL History
Citing Your Mother in Your Research Paper

Andrea S. Libresco

This chapter is for all those secondary teachers who have assigned oral history projects that their students may have enjoyed but somehow did not consider to be real history. It describes how a research paper that invited students to incorporate oral history interviews of their own making proved to be an especially meaningful assignment.

More than a decade ago, I initiated a mini oral history project on immigration in my U.S. history classes by inviting a panel of willing students in the English as a second language (ESL) program to tell their stories to my students. Students from Central and South America, Asia, and Europe told of the conditions in their countries that pushed them away, the conditions in America that pulled them here, the hardships endured on the journey itself, and the receptions they were given upon arrival in America.

My rather sheltered students were shocked to discover that one of their acquaintances, Jorge (not his real name), had seen his fourth-grade teacher shot in front of him and his classmates in El Salvador, had entered the United States concealed in the trunk of a car, and had been treated with a mixture of wariness and derision by more than a few high school students in his early months in this country.

Jorge's oral history and those of other students on the panel clearly moved my students. In class discussion on the day following the presentation, students who had previously seen the immigration question in black and white began to see shades of gray; they softened and sympathized with the immigrant students' plights and indicated that they now felt Jorge should be allowed to stay in the country. The students were willing to let Jorge's brother in as well. Interestingly, their empathy did not extend to anyone not directly related to the teller of this compelling immigration tale; my students would not allow Jorge's neighbors to become legal immigrants.

Because the panel of ESL students had made at least some impression on my history classes, I decided to enlarge the oral history project to give each of my students the opportunity to interview an immigrant and to transcribe and analyze the results. This oral history project met with moderate success. The quality of my students' write-ups improved as their interviewing skills developed; these skills grew further as I organized the assignment to allow for group development of questions, practice interviews, editing, and follow-up interview sessions.

Still, even as their final products improved, I felt there was something missing in the assignment. I realized what it was when one of my students, having completed her oral history project, asked when we would get back to doing *real* history. Even when the end product was a booklet of their immigration stories, my students did not see these stories as a part of history. Finally, through the unlikely vehicle of a mandated eleventh-grade research paper, I found a way to remedy this situation.

My assignment for the research paper retained the oral history portion of the earlier assignment. However, I added to the project an autobiographical novel, *Bread Givers,* by Anzia Yezierska, and a series of primary sources, including sections from Maxine Seller's *Immigrant Women,* Michael Gold's *Jews Without Money,* Thomas Wheeler's *The Immigrant Experience,* and Isaac Metzker's *A Bintel Brief.* In writing their research papers, students were required to use primary sources and were encouraged to include among these sources their own and other students' oral history interviews.

Students had a variety of choices to make within the topic of immigration. Possible questions to be answered by their thesis statements included the following:

- Was the immigrant you interviewed typical of the American (or a particular ethnic group's) immigrant experience?
- Was the American (or a particular ethnic group's) immigrant experience on balance a more positive or more negative one?
- Describe "the anguish of becoming American" for an actual immigrant, a character in *Bread Givers,* and a particular ethnic group.
- Is the experience depicted in *Bread Givers* an accurate reflection of the Jewish and/or American immigrant experience?
- Compare and evaluate past and present immigration policy.

- Compare and evaluate past and present treatment of immigrants by Americans.

- Compare and evaluate the immigrant experiences found in several of the oral histories compiled by you and your classmates.

- Compare *Bread Givers* and a few other fictionalized accounts of the immigrant experience in literature and film to actual immigrant accounts. Possible sources include the oral history of an immigrant or immigrants; secondary sources; current articles and statistics; other novels, such as Mario Puzo's *The Fortunate Pilgrim*, Amy Tan's *The Joy Luck Club*, and Abraham Cahan's *The Rise of David Levinsky*; and films, such as *The Fortunate Pilgrim*, *The Joy Luck Club*, *Hester Street*, *West of Hester Street*, *Avalon*, *Eat a Bowl of Tea*, *The Wedding Banquet*, *El Norte*, and *Mississippi Masala*.

At first, students found the paper difficult to organize because it called for a variety of sources. Quite a few students' early drafts consisted of no more than a standard research paper followed by the oral history write-up. Through individual conferencing and group editing, students came to understand that the fruits of their interviews really were legitimate sources that could be folded into the paper like any other source to help prove their thesis statements. The final results were often compelling.

Christine Winchester, of Irish descent herself, chose Chinese American immigration as her topic. In this excerpt from her paper, she incorporates a piece of an interview with another student into her discussion of how Chinese Americans, because of their physical appearance, are still looked on as "the other."

> In today's world, the Chinese-Americans are not even looked at as American citizens. As one stated: "A third generation American, why must I always be asked how I like living in this country? As if this country never could be my country." (anon. 3) Chinese-Americans, American-born, are asked by strangers if they could speak English. They are even asked when they are returning to their "own" country. (Winchester 9)

Interestingly, the student Christine quoted did not want her comments attributed to her because she feared her classmates would judge her harshly.

Lori Filocamo interviewed her mother and folded her mother's experience into her research on Italian American immigration. As the following excerpts indicate, Lori did not include just one quote in one spot in the paper; rather, she cited her mother throughout, using her as a specific example to support her points about Italian immigration in general. The first excerpt examines push-and-pull factors for immigration.

America offered many Italians what Italy denied them, such as good soil for farming, high pay for their work, low taxes on their earnings, no compulsory military service and greater personal freedom. "We are now able to work and live together as a family, instead of being scattered around the world to make a living. After our first relatives came to America and established themselves here, they saved up enough money to send the rest of the family overseas." (Filocamo 1997, 2)

The second excerpt discusses the difficulty in learning English for Italian immigrants.

The typical immigrant to North America during this period was a young man with little formal education from his homeland and he often spoke broken English. "Things were difficult when we first came here but we seemed to manage. Even though I didn't know a word of English, through work and my friends from the neighborhood, I began speaking broken English." (3)

Although Lori needs to make the transition between the experience of the typical turn-of-the-century immigrant and the experience of her mother in the 1960s, she has clearly used her mother as a real source to support her point about learning the language as a recent immigrant.

The final excerpt quoted here from Lori's paper compares women's roles in the Old Country to those in America.

Women were also employed in the garment industry. Josephine Costanzo described her mother working in a mill: "My mother was a twister in the Lawrence mills. It was unusual; in Italy there were no jobs for women. In fact, people that heard about it back in the village didn't like the idea of women working. But my mother felt she was doing no different from all the women, so she decided to work. Make some money." (Hoobler 1991, 55) In Italy, women did not go out for work; they stayed in the house and did house work; nothing else was accepted: "Back in my hometown, the women were always expected to do the house cleaning and the cooking for the family, while the men worked outside on the garden and took care of the animals." (Filocamo 1997, 1)

Although I suspect Lori did not consciously process her paper this way, she seamlessly uses a primary source cited by a "real" historian and then makes the same point using her mother as primary source and Lori as the historian quoting her.

The final example of student work cited here is by Al'ai Flores, a very recent immigrant from the Philippines. He arrived in December 1996, about a month before we began working on the oral histories. This excerpt uses his own mother's experience of the lack of job possibilities in the Philippines to show the pull of America as a land of economic opportunity.

> Regarding the unemployment in the Philippines, Yale graduate writer Knoll said, "The *Manila Times* summarizes the appeal of America: "The migrating Filipino sees no opportunity for him in the Philippines. Advertise in a Manila paper and offer a job . . . And you will get a thousand applicants. Make the same offer in any provincial town, and the response will be twice as much." (Knoll 1982, 90) Clearly, this means that unemployment in the Philippines during that time was very high. No wonder my mother said in an interview, "I couldn't find a job anywhere. It took me three years to find a nursing job after my graduation and the salary offered was very small. It's not even 25% of my monthly salary here. While even when I was still in the Philippines, I was already hired by a U.S. Hospital here in new York." (Flores 1997, 1) From this, the difference between the salary and demands in employment in the Philippines and here in the United States can be inferred.

The act of citing their own interviews and those of their classmates had done what my previous oral history assignments had failed to do: it showed students that their stories were part of the sweep of real history. Doing the research paper gave them the skills of a historian; using their own primary sources made them and their families actors on the historical stage.

This project addressed NCSS standards (1) Culture and (4) Individual Development and Identity. It also met the national history standards in its encouragement of chronological thinking, or the need to distinguish between past, present, and future time. Historical comprehension was fostered by the need to read narratives imaginatively. Most significant, by formulating historical questions and heeding perspectives of time and place, students began to develop historical research capabilities. Cultivating skills for identifying issues and problems in the past enabled students to engage in analysis of historical issues as well as decision making.

Historians have an interest in examining the progression of immigrants from ethnicity to acculturation to assimilation and in understanding how this process occurs over generations. Teachers and students can extend an oral history process such as this one to make it even more ambitious, encouraging research and analysis that even more closely approximates the work of historians.

One way of extending this assignment would be to give it more of a generational focus. Going beyond "citing your mother," students could interview grandparents and even great-grandparents (through the verbal recollections of succeeding generations). The purpose of such generational inquiries would be to assess change over time, to examine how

things were, how they ceased to be what they had been, how they became something different, and with what consequences.

Students who investigate generational developments could make a
cost-benefit assessment using a number of variables to determine
changes that people consider beneficial to their lives and those of their
families and changes that entail some sense of loss. One could examine
how the immigrant generation evaluates its experience in the United
States (several of the student essays referred to in this article began to
approach this). Establishing a set of relevant variables that can be examined over generations can help show how events in the past affected
individuals, how particular individuals interpreted the significance of
those events to their lives, and how perspectives on events change
over time.

Students' interviews could seek to determine how job patterns in
a family changed or remained the same over time; to what extent
the level of education increased; how the quality of life changed as
gauged by income, home ownership (a key component of the American Dream), and residential patterns (ability to move out of ghetto-type
areas into places of more diversity); and to what extent immigrants
and their descendants retained or lost their original language, culture,
and religious practices. Students could also inquire about the extent to
which the immigrants and their children experienced prejudice and
discrimination or held negative views of other groups themselves.

If a student finds it more comfortable to conduct an inquiry of
neighbors or other community members rather than of family, that
would be entirely appropriate and can provide the same kind of generational analysis. Finally, students can seek to take stock of how they see
themselves as the present generation in the context of the unfolding
events, choices, and consequences that have affected those who pre-
ceded them.

Immigration historian Michael D'Innocenzo points out that American society has been the most change-oriented society in the history
of the world. He adds that we often confuse change with progress, not-
ing that while there can be no progress without change, not all change
results in progress. I like to think that if my students take away from
this assignment the realization that what their families did mattered in
history, then they may come to realize that what they do with their
lives will matter as well.

Teaching Sources

The following sources are used in the classroom or appear in the excerpts from student papers.

Cahan, A. 1960. *The Rise of David Levinsky.* New York: Harper & Row.

D'Innocenzo, M., and J. P. Sirefman, eds. 1992. *Immigration and Ethnicity: American Society—"Melting Pot" or "Salad Bowl"?* Westport, CT: Greenwood.

Filocamo, L. 1997. Interview with Maria Filocamo. 1 April.

Flores, A. 1997. Interview with Celina Lee. 27 April.

Gold, M. 1930. *Jews Without Money.* New York: H. Liverright.

Hoobler, D. 1991. *The Italian American Family Album.* New York: Oxford University Press.

Knoll, T. 1982. *Becoming Americans.* Portland, OR: Coast to Coast.

Metzker, I., ed. 1971. *A Bintel Brief.* New York: Ballantine.

Puzo, M. 1964. *The Fortunate Pilgrim.* Greenwich, CT: Fawcett.

Seller, M. S., ed. 1994. *Immigrant Women.* Albany, NY: SUNY Press.

Tan, A. 1989. *The Joy Luck Club.* New York: Ivy.

Wheeler, T. 1971. *The Immigrant Experience.* New York: Penguin.

Yezierska, A. 1975. *Bread Givers.* New York: George Braziller.

Note

Andrea S. Libresco teaches American and global history at Oceanside High School and is lead teacher for elementary social studies in the Oceanside, New York, school district. She also teaches Social Studies Methods at Hofstra University in Hempstead, New York. She was named Long Island Secondary Social Studies Teacher of the Year in May 1997.

Appendix A: The Turner Thesis

These excerpts are from "The Significance of the Frontier in American History,"
an address delivered by Frederick Jackson Turner to the American Historical
Association meeting in Chicago on July 12, 1893. This was the year of the
World's Columbian Exposition in Chicago, which opened on May 1 and closed
on October 30. It was also the year of the Cherokee Outlet land rush (the largest
of five land runs on Indian Territory in Oklahoma), which opened and closed
on September 16.

In a recent bulletin of the Superintendent of the Census for 1890 appear these significant words: "Up to and including 1880 the country had a frontier of settlement, but at present the unsettled area has been so broken into by isolated bodies of settlement that there can hardly be said to be a frontier line. In the discussion of its extent, its westward movement, etc, it can not, therefore, any longer have a place in the census reports." This brief official statement marks the closing of a great historic movement. Up to our own day American history has been in a large degree the history of the colonization of the Great West. The existence of an area of free land, its continuous recession, and the advance of American settlement westward, explain American development.

. . . American social development has been continually beginning over again on the frontier. This perennial rebirth, this fluidity of American life, this expansion westward with its new opportunities, its continuous touch with the simplicity of primitive society, furnish the forces dominating American character.

. . . The most significant thing about the American frontier is, that it lies at the hither edge of free land. In the census reports it is treated as the margin of that settlement which has a density of two or more to the square mile. The term is an elastic one, and for our purposes does not need sharp definition. We shall consider the whole frontier belt including the Indian country and the outer margin of the "settled area" of the census reports.

. . . The frontier is the line of most rapid and effective Americanization. The wilderness masters the colonist. It finds him a European in dress, industries, tools, modes of travel, and thought. It takes him from the railroad car and puts him in the birch canoe. It strips off the garments of civilization and arrays him in the hunting shirt and the moccasin. It puts him in the log cabin of the Cherokee and Iroquois and runs an Indian palisade around him. Before long he has gone to planting Indian corn and plowing with a sharp stick, he shouts the war cry and takes the scalp in orthodox Indian fashion. In short, at the frontier the environment is at first too strong for the man. He must accept the conditions which it furnishes, or perish, and so he fits himself into the Indian clearings and follows the Indian trails.

. . . In the middle of this century . . . the distinctive frontier of the period is found in California, where the gold discoveries had sent a sudden tide of adventurous miners, and in Oregon, and the settlements in Utah . . . so now the settlers beyond the Rocky Mountains needed means of communication with the East, and in the furnishings of these arose the settlement of the Great Plains and the development of still another kind of frontier life. Railroads, fostered by land grants, sent an increasing tide of immigrants into the far West. The United States Army fought a series of Indian wars in Minnesota, Dakota, and the Indian Territory.

. . . The United States lies like a huge page in the history of society. Line by line as we read this continental page from West to East we find the record of social evolution. It begins with the Indian and the hunter, it goes on to tell of the disintegration of savagery by the entrance of the trader, the pathfinder of civilization; we read the annals of the pastoral stage in ranch life, the exploitation of the soil by the raising of unrotated crops of corn and wheat in sparsely settled farming communities; the intensive culture of the denser farm settlement; and finally the manufacturing organization with city and factory system.

. . . Stand at Cumberland Gap and watch the procession of civilization, marching single file—the buffalo following the trail to the salt springs, the Indian, the fur trader and hunter, the cattle-raiser, the pioneer farmer—and the frontier has passed by.

. . . Why was it that the Indian trader passed so rapidly across the continent? . . . The explanation of the rapidity of this advance is connected with the effects of the trader on the Indian. The trading post left the unarmed tribes at the mercy of those that had purchased firearms . . . Thus the disintegrating forces of civilization entered the wilderness. Every river valley and Indian trail became a fissure in Indian society, and so that society became honeycombed. Long before the pioneer farmer appeared on the scene, primitive Indian life had passed away. The farmers met Indians armed with guns. The trading frontier, while steadily undermining Indian power by making the tribes ultimately dependent on the whites, yet, through its sale of guns, gave to the Indians increased power of resistance to the farming frontier.

. . . The Indian trade pioneered the way for civilization. The buffalo trail became the Indian trail and this became the trader's "trace," the trails widened into roads, and the roads into turnpikes, and these in turn were transformed into railroads . . . In this progress from savage conditions lie topics of the evolutionist.

. . . The effect of the Indian frontier as a consolidating agent in our history is important . . . in this connection may be mentioned the importance of the frontier, from that day to this, as a military training school, keeping alive the power of resistance to aggression, and developing the stalwart and rugged qualities of the frontiersman . . . The frontier army post, serving to protect the settlers from the Indians, has also acted as a wedge to open the Indian country, and has been a nucleus for settlement.

. . . The public domain has been a force of profound importance in the nationalization and development of the government . . . The purchase of Louisiana was perhaps the constitutional turning point in the history of the Republic, inasmuch as it afforded both a new area for national legislation and the occasion of the down fall of the policy of strict construction.

. . . But the most important effect of the frontier has been in the promotion of democracy here and in Europe. As has been indicated, the frontier is productive of individualism . . . The frontier states that came into the Union in the first quarter of a century of its existence came in with democrating suffrage provisions, and had reactive effects of the highest importance upon the older States whose peoples were being attracted there.

. . . The result is that to the frontier the American intellect owes its striking characteristics. That coarseness and strength combined with acuteness and inquisitiveness; that practical, inventive turn of mind, quick to find expedients; that masterful grasp of material things, lacking in the artistic but powerful to effect great ends; that restless, nervous energy; that dominant individualism, working for good and evil, and withal that buoyancy and exuberance which comes with freedom—these are the traits of the frontier, or traits called out elsewhere because of the existence of the frontier.

. . . And now, four centuries from the discovery of America, at the end of a hundred years of life under the Constitution, the frontier has gone, and with its going has closed the first period of American history.

Note

Turner's speech as it appeared in the *Report of the American Historical Association for 1893* can be found on the web at <xroads.virginia.edu/~HYPER/TURNER/chapter 1.html>.